Praise for Croissants vs. Bagels

"Robbie's inclusive approach to networking is what makes him so effective at building relationships. *Croissants vs. Bagels* is a powerful concept that will forever change your approach to networking. Follow his techniques so you can build your own strong professional network."

—Dorie Clark, best-selling author of
Reinventing You and *Stand Out*

"Life gets busy and we're not always as prepared as we'd like to be heading into a conference. This book will help you take advantage of small networking moments at the event—like chatting with other early arrivals at your breakout session and waving over people to join your lunch table."

—Thom Singer, CSP aka "Conference Catalyst,"
author of twelve books on the power of business
relationships, networking, and presentation skills,
including *The ABCs of Networking*

"Have you ever wondered what to do at a crowded networking event? Not know what to do or say? Then you will really enjoy Robbie's practical steps to navigating a room and making great connections. Whether you are a nervous first-time attendee or have been going for years you will learn valuable takeaways to give (and get) attention of the people you meet."

—Neen James, Keynote Speaker, and
author of *Folding Time* and *Attention Pays*

D1648735

"No one works a conference like Robbie—an artist of networking. Robbie gets the relational and the practical. This book is pocket-sized wisdom to help you make the most of conferences. Tips like writing your follow-up email draft in advance, using specific programs to keep track of priority business cards, and strategies for actually following up after the event despite having a busy life. Robbie covers it all."

—Rea Carey, executive director of
the National LGBTQ Task Force,
host of the Creating Change Conference

"One lesson I learned while working my way up from baggage handler to CEO—relationships matter. We can't rely on technology to help us make those connections, we need to take advantage of opportunities to meet in person. This book will help you do just that."

—Howard Putnam, former CEO of
Southwest Air and professional speaker

"By taking the 'work' out of 'networking,' Robbie redefines what it means to network and build meaningful relationships that can help you achieve your goals."

—Jeffrey Hayzlett, a global business celebrity,
best-selling business author, and
award-winning public speaker

"Robbie offers wonderful wisdom in this book—read it not only for important lessons about how to network at conferences and grow your career, but how to approach life with courage and an inclusive spirit."

—Greg M. Epstein, Humanist Chaplain
at Harvard University

CROISSANTS
vs. BAGELS

STRATEGIC, EFFECTIVE & INCLUSIVE
NETWORKING AT CONFERENCES

ROBBIE SAMUELS

Thank you for purchasing the
print version of this book,
I'm bundling it with the audio
book at no extra charge.

Download at www.RobbieSamuels.com/audiobook

For my wife Jess Samuels,
for her unyielding love and support.

Contents

INTRODUCTION

CONGRATULATIONS!

You are prioritizing building relationships to excel in your career or business. Even so, you might have some anxiety around doing all of this—for many, the idea of meeting with strangers ranks somewhere around the thrill of getting a root canal. Some people don't find it anxiety provoking but feel the time they spend at networking events isn't effective and they would rather just put their head down and do their work. Perhaps you have even felt the desire to avoid conferences and networking events altogether.

Meeting the right people has been critical to your success and you know your business or career will grow if you continue to make the right kinds of connections. Despite knowing this, you feel exhausted just thinking about going to yet another networking event with those tight networking circles.

The title of this book is *Croissants vs. Bagels* because the shape of these breakfast foods are a metaphor for those tight networking circles—bagels—and what happens if someone opens up their body language to let you in to the group—croissants. If this were a common practice, networking events would feel more inclusive and easier to navigate.

I believe what sets this book apart from other books about networking is the focus on being inclusive. If you want to be truly effective, you'll need to be inclusive when networking. In practice, being inclusive means being thoughtful about the questions we ask, being aware of how our body language makes us easier or harder to approach, and overall having a host mentality.

Bottom line, I wrote this book to help you stop wasting time networking and be more strategic, effective, and inclusive when building relationships.

YES, WE'RE TALKING ABOUT NETWORKING

WHAT DO YOU THINK OF WHEN YOU HEAR THE WORD "NETWORKING"?

If you are like most people, based on your experience at events the word "networking" has a negative connotation. If you believe going to networking events is not a good use of your time, but continue attending events without changing your strategy, well, it's like Einstein said, "The definition of insanity is doing the same thing over and over and expecting a different result."

A New Definition of Networking

You need a new definition of networking, not one based on transactional exchanges with strangers. This limited definition isn't working for you and won't get you the results you want. This book will help you reframe what's possible when you make the effort to leave the comfort of your home to meet people in-person.

"What's in it for me?"

You probably have experienced meeting people who have the phrase, "What's in it for me?" top of mind when they are at a networking event. If someone were to approach you with this frame of mind, it would seem like they were quickly screening you to see if you were worth their attention and if they then acted chummy there was something they needed from you. Even if you offered something of value, you wouldn't feel a meaningful bond with this person or the desire to stay connected.

The Dirty Business of Networking

In a 2014 Harvard study, researchers found this type of "instrumental networking" made people feel dirty.[1] Individuals who felt this way then avoided networking, and it had an adverse impact on their job performance.

This book will help you shift from a transactional

approach to a new definition of networking, where you achieve your goals by building great relationships.

COMMON COMPLAINTS AROUND NETWORKING

MEETING STRANGERS IS SCARY

Unless you are a hermit, you have a lot of experience meeting people. In fact, some of your closest friends started out as strangers. You met while playing ball together as kids (or adults), at a neighborhood block party, when you were volunteering, at your best friend's wedding, working together, or at a bar one night while out with friends. You know how to do this. You have met strangers who became active connections in your life. Networking is meeting people and staying in touch, and doesn't have to happen only at "networking events." With some planning and goal setting, you will be able to build on your previous experience and become more successful at "networking."

NETWORKING IS EXHAUSTING

There are many reasons you may be experiencing this. The main one is you haven't seen results from going to endless events and meetings. So, of course, repeating the same thing over and over again will feel exhausting and pointless. You may also find it draining to be around people and you recharge best when you are alone. If so, then you likely identify as an introvert on the Myers-Briggs scale. What if you could attend an event for just one hour and leave feeling like you had accomplished your networking goals? It is possible when you know your purpose in attending a particular event and have set goals, which keep you circulating during the first hour.

IT'S A WASTE OF TIME

Extroverts, on the other end of the Myers-Briggs scale, get energized being around people. So they won't find networking exhausting, but may still feel like it is a waste of their time. If you attend three or more events a month, or perhaps even three or more a week, then you would expect to see results from all of your effort. Without a solid plan in place, attending scattershot events and buzzing around the room making small talk will leave you wondering if it's all worth it.

Collecting stacks of business cards each month is not the point of attending these events. Having a clear sense of purpose and specific goals will help you make the most of these encounters and you'll become a sought-after attendee when you know how to use your extroverted personality to help others connect and feel welcomed in the room.

STRATEGIC. EFFECTIVE. INCLUSIVE?

This book was written to help you be more strategic, effective, and inclusive when networking. It makes sense you would want to be more strategic and effective, but you may be wondering what being inclusive has to do with networking.

OTHERING AND ONLINESS

You are not alone if you have ever walked into an event where you didn't know anyone, circled the room, and felt like you didn't belong. You look around, and everyone else seems to be chatting as if they are best friends, but you are feeling like the only odd one out in the room. This feeling of onliness (pronounced only-ness) is exacerbated when someone starts a conversation with you by making an observation or asking a curious question about your appearance – the kind of comment often made when people meet you for the first time. They've noticed something different about you and have singled it out by commenting on it.

In this book, I will give very specific examples of how to avoid comments and questions resulting in this kind of *othering*—treating somebody as "not one of us." If you are trying to be effective when networking you will want to avoid these awkward moments—which inevitably make it difficult to build a real connection.

Being a Host

Inclusion is not just about avoiding awkward questions or wrong assumptions; it is also about being a good host and connector. If you attend an organization's events frequently enough to be considered a regular, you will become known by other regulars. Being a regular will help you get into conversations with other regulars and also be a connector, which will help you engage newcomers in the room. In this book, I will share different ways you can take on the role of host, even if you had nothing to do with scheduling the event. Meeting professionals and event organizers can ask regulars to step into a host role, thereby helping others make connections in the room and also helping with retention of regulars. We will explore this win-win strategy in more detail in this book.

Body Language

We have all seen those tight networking circles, when everyone else in the room seems like they are engrossed in a group conversation, and you are the one left out. On an individual level, you can begin to shift the culture of an event by being intentionally open in your body language.

Event organizers can use this information to train their long-time attendees, volunteers, board members, and staff—and the improved ease of moving in and out of conversations will be felt by everyone in attendance.

This book includes diagrams to help you improve your stance, so you will become easier to approach and will be less likely to be stuck in a conversation. This concept is called "croissants vs. bagels" and has been the most memorable takeaway from Art of the Schmooze, my signature presentation—and thus, the title of this book.

What to Expect in this Book

The world revolves around relationships and the power of our networks. This book will inspire you to get out of your comfort zone and meet new people. To do this, I will be sharing specific examples of what to do and what not to do.

Full Disclosure

I'm an outgoing extrovert who loves to convene people and organize events. I'm well aware of the privilege I experience as an outgoing extrovert—it takes very little effort for me to speak with strangers and I recharge around lots of people. I will be sharing many tips to help shy and/or introverted people be seen, heard, and respected when they attend events and conferences, without having to transform themselves into outgoing extroverts. I'm also going to be encouraging my fellow outgoing extroverts to step into a host role whenever possible, so they use their ease in the room to help others feel welcomed.

Don't Do This

I'm certain you have experienced bad networking techniques: Sharks who are only there to meet their own needs and have nothing to offer. Pushy people who talk too much and show little interest in others. Curious questioners who make others feel like outsiders, creating an unwelcome environment. In this book, you'll learn valuable lessons from each of these scenarios.

Networking Can Take Place Anywhere

Focusing your effort only on "networking events" will result in you missing a lot of potential connections. Practice your approach when the stakes aren't as high to feel more confident when you have the opportunity to meet influencers in your field.

You can make great connections when you least expect it: at the Starbucks in the conference hotel, while at jury duty, at a professional development training, or at an author event. Conferences in particular offer many opportunities to meet recognized experts in your field and strengthen your professional network. This book will help you be prepared to take advantage of these big and small networking moments.

Ways Networking Can Help You

Job-hunting is one of the top reasons people say they need to network. If you limit your job search to leads from your closest family and friends, and they can't help you, you will not be successful. If you are in sales or fundraising, you will need to leave your office to meet potential clients and prospective donors. Once you reframe networking as relationship building, you will realize the unlimited potential. As a new parent, you will be able to build community with other new parents. You'll be able to find support for the causes you care about and inspire others to volunteer with you. This book will help you reframe networking so you can realize the potential all around you.

Why Focus on Conferences?

First and foremost, attending conferences is an investment in yourself. If you are serious about getting ahead in your career and making great connections in your field, then invest in yourself by attending a conference. Yes, you'll be taking precious time away from work—and home—and sometimes the cost to attend will come out of your pocket. You will want to be certain you make a big return on your investment (ROI).

Learning opportunities are everywhere you look these days: blogs, podcasts, webinars, YouTube, and just by scrolling through Twitter. You might be wondering then, why anyone would spend considerable time and money attending a conference. It's true, content is everywhere, but none of the virtual methods of consuming content can match the benefits of an in-person event.

Here are some ways you can increase your return on investment (ROI) at conferences:

TAKEAWAYS

The best conferences will challenge you as a person and as a professional. You'll come home re-energized and full of new ideas. Takeaways could include learning new skills, being reminded of best practices, the serendipity of discovering a great new app, or learning a new way of solving an old problem.

NEW POINT OF VIEW

While you could learn new skills online, you will be more open to new ideas when you're out of your usual day-to-day spaces. You've experienced this when your staff held an off-site meeting or retreat. Being in a new space can get you out of your rut and open to new experiences, leading to more takeaways to help you grow your career or business.

NETWORKING

Meet the people whose work inspires you, meet your competition, meet people to be in a mastermind group with or to join your personal board of directors—this is what's possible if you attend a conference.

Most people are not natural networkers, and going to large events will likely be outside your comfort zone. You understand the importance of networking at conferences, but you haven't always felt like you make the most of these opportunities. You may even think they are a waste of your time and you would be more productive staying home instead of leaving the office for a few days to attend a conference.

Year after year you attend many events, conferences, and conventions. You collect dozens of business cards at each of these events and bring them back to the office with good intentions. You place these business cards next to your keyboard and later in the week you move them, adding them to the pile you have in the back corner of your desk.

In a few months, you decide it's time for spring cleaning and move all these business cards—neatly stacked, of course—into a drawer. A year later you find them in your drawer, you're not able to remember where they were from or what follow-up you had done or planned to do, so you recycle them. And then you head right back out to another event and start the exhausting cycle all over again.

There is a difference between collecting business cards and building relationships.

In an age where information is one click away, and we count "likes" as engagement, conferences hold the promise of meaningful in-person connections with like-minded colleagues. Only through strategic planning will this promise become a reality.

READY TO TAKE ACTION? YEAH!

I would love to hear what resonates with you in this book - especially what made you say "yeah!" Email yeah@croissantsvsbagels.com to let me know how this book has inspired you to take action. I am grateful to my launch team for sharing their "yeah!" moments and I can't wait to hear yours.

BE STRATEGIC

STRATEGY STARTS WITH MINDSET

If you do all the planning and your head isn't convinced it will be worth your time, it won't work out. If you believe highly successful people won't want to speak to you or if you fear *no one* will want to talk with you, well, it probably won't be a great event for you.

If you have a "what's in it for me?" attitude, you aren't going to be successful.

Jeffrey Hayzlett, a global business celebrity, best-selling business author, and award-winning public speaker, has a huge following. On Twitter alone he has over six hundred thousand followers. He needs a team to get him from his hotel room to business meetings at major conventions, because so many people want to stop him to say hello and take a selfie with him.

And yet, his base was not built artificially through ads, but by asking, "What can I do to help you?" His servant leadership and belief in adding value to his network has helped him be successful.

Becoming successful didn't change his approach to networking. He has always had this abundant way of engaging and continues to be approachable. "I try to be accessible, no matter who you are," said Jeffrey.[2]

His philosophy is something for all of us to consider: to be sure we retain our core sense of self, our openness to people and their ideas, as we climb our career ladder.

POWER DYNAMICS

Dr. Josh Packard, the Executive Director of Social Research Lab at University of Northern Colorado, does not have the reach or influence Jeffrey has, but he approaches networking in a similar way. Instead of thinking, "What's in it for me?" he has a powerful reframe. He begins by asking himself, "What does this person need from me at this moment?"[3]

Asking this question helped him avoid feeling like he was asking for something from people who were more senior than him. The power dynamics shifted when he realized there was something he could offer in return.

By approaching networking in this way, it doesn't feel like "instrumental networking," and he is less likely to experience the negative feelings often felt by people who are still climbing their career ladder.

I've always advised that networking becomes relationship building when you offer before you ask. You can be creative in what you offer.

What Can You Offer?

So before we dive into strategies, let's take a moment to reflect on the many ways you can provide value to highly successful people. The truth is, no matter how successful someone is, they will have areas in their life where they still need support.

The offer could be a lead on a qualified vendor or a book publisher. It could be help with social media strategy or sharing a productivity tech tip.

A great offer is when your skills and experience are a match for what they need. Don't undersell yourself and the value you can add.

It's also a good idea to "get on their stage" before the event by sharing their social media posts and commenting on their blog posts. If your name is familiar when you meet in person, the highly successful person will be more inclined to have a conversation, and you will be more confident when speaking with them.

Keep in mind; if you develop relationships with people still growing in their career, those connections will be strong when they become leaders in your field.

Mindset Isn't Everything

Conferences are expensive and time intensive, but I wouldn't recommend avoiding them altogether. What you need is a strategy to boost your confidence and ensure you are using your time and money wisely.

To be strategic, you need to have a plan. To have a plan, you need to do some research. Before doing anything, you need to get very clear on why this conference is the particular event you should be attending. If you only attend because you "have to" and don't put any effort into a strategic plan, then it's likely you will not feel the event was valuable enough for the time you spent there.

It's important for you to have a strategy and a sense of purpose. You should be able to answer these kinds of questions:

- Why this event? Out of all the possible events to attend, why this one?

- What do you hope to learn?

- What inspiration are you looking for?

- Who do you want to meet?

Answer these questions by doing some research and aligning this event with your personal/professional goals.

SETTING GOALS

You will want to set personal goals for how many people you want to meet and the number of reconnections you want to have. You need to do both. If you only collect new business cards, you're not deepening connections with the people you already have met. If you only speak to people you know, you are missing out on one of the best reasons to attend conferences: expanding your professional network.

Some people are shyer and/or more introverted, so having goals helps them keep mingling. Individuals who are outgoing and/or extroverted may already be great at "working a room" but may need to set personal goals to be sure they have meaningful connections and not just quick handshakes and hugs with everyone they see.

SHY AND/OR INTROVERTED?

A moment ago, I said "shy and/or introverted." These terms are often conflated, but being outgoing doesn't automatically mean you are an extrovert (and introverts aren't always shy). These are two different scales and are not directly correlated.

Extraversion and introversion, as measured by the Myers-Briggs Personality Test, is about where you draw your energy. Do you get recharged being around lots of people or being home alone? Not everyone is distinctly an extrovert or introvert. Many people will fall somewhere in between. If you fall right in the middle, you might identify as an ambivert.

A separate question is whether you are outgoing or shy. If you are a social butterfly who can talk to just about anyone, you probably identify as outgoing. Wallflower in new social situations? You probably identify as shy.

ARE YOU AN OUTGOING INTROVERT?
OR A SHY EXTROVERT?

Some introverts are naturally very outgoing or have learned to be more outgoing because their job requires it. They are often mistaken for extroverts, but they find socializing draining.

On the other hand, some individuals are recharged by being around lots of people but are quite shy. These shy extroverts enjoy going out but tend to hang on the edges of the room. They hate being the center of attention and are assumed to be introverts.

Wherever you fall on these two scales, I want you to engage with other people in the room more easily so the energy you put into the experience is rewarded by great connections.

SET "STRETCH GOALS" FOR THIS EVENT

If you're more of a wallflower, make an effort to meet three new people and reconnect with three people you know. For those of you who are social butterflies, meeting three new people might be your goal for each day of the conference; just be sure you have meaningful connections. This means having engaging conversations and not just handshaking, hugging, or air kissing your way through the crowd. Be certain to make a connection, not stopping to chat only long enough to shake hands and collect a business card.

Were you inspired by one of the main stage speakers? Tweet at them or send them a LinkedIn message. Ask to meet up while at the conference. I've done this and can tell you it works. I ended up meeting the former CEO of Southwest Airlines by sending him a LinkedIn message during the event. Later he was a guest on my podcast, On the Schmooze (www.OntheSchmooze.com).

You never know unless you say hello.

PREP FOR SUCCESS

WHO WILL BE THERE?
A good place to start prepping for any event would be to figure out who will be there—either the attendee list or in general who has attended in the past. If you know someone who has attended this conference, you can ask their advice about whether it would be a good fit.

Even if you can't access the attendee list, you'll know who is on the host committee or organizing team, who is presenting, and who is receiving an award. All of this will help you determine if this is the right event for you and if there are particular people you'd like to meet.

RESEARCH

Once you've identified who might be attending and created a short list of people you'd like to meet, use LinkedIn to learn more about them before you go to the event. Unless you turn off the default, people will know you are looking at their profiles. This can be very beneficial, as it may lead to them looking at your profile. So be sure your LinkedIn profile is up-to-date and your photo will help them easily identify you.

TWITTER

A couple of weeks before the conference pay attention to the Twitter hashtag for the event. People will start to post and the volume and frequency of tweets will increase as you get closer to the event.

Retweet information shared by the conference team and anyone else who catches your eye. Some people are very active on Twitter leading up to and during the event. You'll get on their radar by retweeting their content throughout the event and can reply via Twitter to invite them to meet up.

FACEBOOK

Many conferences have a Facebook group. Start to pay closer attention to the posts a few weeks before the event and actively participate by liking and commenting.

Share advice, comment on an interesting article, or post a question. Be present, engaged and notice who is posting and commenting most frequently. Learn a little bit more about the active posters and then reach out with an invitation to connect before the event (via phone or video chat) or invite them to meet at the event.

These online communities are a great way to stay engaged after the event as well.

REACH OUT

Have you just stumbled across a very promising contact? Someone you want to be certain you cross paths with at the event? Why not reach out to them beforehand and invite them to meet for coffee or a quick chat in the hallway? Even if you aren't able to set up a specific time to meet, your initiative will make you stand out.

As you are doing your research about the event, you might come across a session you are really excited about attending. Reach out to the presenter to let them know you are looking forward to their session. Be specific about what in particular drew you to the topic and include a question you hope they will address. Then, when you meet them at the event, mention you had reached out beforehand—and send them a follow-up email right after their session. This helps to get you on their radar and more open to chatting or meeting during the conference.

Host a Private Dinner

One reason for reaching out ahead of time is to invite someone to a private dinner you are hosting at the conference. If you are looking to build a stronger professional network, hosting your own event is an option you should not overlook. This may seem like too much work, but the benefits far outweigh the effort.

This strategy has been a great way to network for John Corcoran, an attorney, former Clinton White House Writer, host of Smart Business Revolution podcast, and co-founder of Rise25 Inner Circle. John said, "You don't need to be the most connected person in the world to do this. They are not coming just for you. You bring together a group of people, they will come for the group. Start by inviting a couple of people, and pretty soon they'll say, 'Wow, look at all of these different people coming.'"[4]

Introverts in particular would benefit from hosting a private dinner. Convening people and being a host allows you to have smaller group and one-on-one connections. The pressure is not on you. Once you bring people together, they are excited to be in with each other and find shared interests. You get the benefit of being recognized as the connector, without having to know everyone's life story at the table.

Set up this dinner in advance and confirm a couple of guests before the event takes place. In the "Resources" section, I've outlined the steps to hosting a private dinner at a conference.

RELATIONSHIPS ARE BUILT OVER TIME

Consider for a moment the stack of business cards you've collected from the events you've attended over the last three to six months. Some of those connections were a great fit for the work you're doing right now, so you've stayed in touch, but a vast majority of those new contacts might not have received a follow-up email. If there isn't a purpose tied to following up, doing so can quickly fall to the bottom of a long to-do list.

Some of those new contacts would be valuable and lead to significant relationships, but a one-time meeting at a loud networking event isn't enough of a catalyst. By hosting a dinner, you are creating an opportunity for you to deepen the relationship.

The benefits to hosting your own event aren't limited to you; your guests will benefit from the introductions they make through you.

Start with Follow Up

You have the right mindset, you've done some research, and you are committed to attending a particular event. The next step is to draft your follow-up email. Yes, BEFORE you leave for the event, write your follow-up email. Writing your follow-up message will require you to get clear on who you want to meet, either specifically or in general, and what you'd want to talk about with them.

Drafting this email will also help you think through your elevator pitch and personalize it for this event. In the "Resources" section, I've included step-by-step details to write this email and strategies for using it effectively.

Most people are not very good at follow up. They amass business cards, but collecting business cards is not the goal of networking. The goal is to build relationships, that requires connecting after the event.

Track Priority Business Cards

The other piece of this is keeping track of the business cards you collect so you can prioritize how you spend your time following up. To keep track, turn down a corner of the business card so it stands out when you are sorting through all the cards you received. Write a note on the back of the card, it will remind you where/when you met, what you had discussed, and what resource you (or they) had agreed to send.

Follow up will be a breeze, if you write your email ahead of time and track the cards you want to prioritize.

ACTUALLY MEET PEOPLE

Of course, this advice only works if you approach people while at the conference. If you lurk on the sides of the room or bury your nose in your phone while waiting for the presenter to start the next breakout session, you are missing out on the opportunities around you.

Conferences hold the promise of in-person connection with like-minded colleagues. This promise becomes real if you have a strategy and actually meet people.

LOOK FOR CROISSANTS

Since you've done your research you know this is a great event to meet potential clients, meet leaders in your field, or find people to invite to your mastermind group. So now you need to go over and talk to the tight networking circle over there. Yeah, the huddle where everyone is standing shoulder-to-shoulder and no one is noticing you standing nearby.

I know, I know—not easy to do. Okay, so before trying to tackle one of those hard to break into networking circles (which I call "bagels"), look for groups with a bit of an opening. Those are the "croissants" you are seeking so you can more easily join their conversation.

In the "Be Inclusive" section I share more details about my "croissants vs. bagels" networking concept, including diagrams to help you get the best foot positioning to open your body language and invite people to connect with you.

"What Do You Do?"

I also recommend prepping an answer to the ubiquitous, "What do you do?" question (which I urge people to stop asking). Instead of saying your company and job title, try something like "I help ___ do ___," or "I inspire __ to do ___." Play around with different responses and see what works for you. Have a couple of quick stories ready to illustrate the positive impact your work has on the world.

For instance, if you are a consultant who works with sales teams, you could answer with, "Through innovative training, I inspire sales teams to reach and exceed their goals." If you are a divorce lawyer, you could answer with, "I guide my clients through the difficult process of divorce, while achieving equitable outcomes."

Notice how different those responses are from simply saying, "I'm a consultant," or "I'm a lawyer." The longer responses invite questions and could lead to further conversation, while the shorter responses may not.

Going into an event with this prep work done will help you feel more confident, and based on your research you will know there are a lot of people you hope to meet. You will make the most of the opportunity to engage with people in person and do the follow-up leading to further connections down the road.

You will stop wasting time networking and start building great relationships. You will have a strong sense of purpose, and be able to judge if you were successful.

How to Stand Out

Another strategy at conferences is to stand out from the crowd so you can attract people you'd like to meet.

Rather than having to go up to strangers and try to find common ground, people will come up to you knowing they have something in common with you.

Having people come to you is easier than having to figure out who to speak with at a conference, so this is an especially good plan for introverts who want to maximize their engagement while expending less energy.

VOLUNTEER

When I first started to attend large conferences, I signed up to volunteer for the first couple of years. Volunteering was an excellent way to meet the organizers and be recognized for my willingness to help out in any way. Years later I was hired to work on the conference team because the conference director remembered me.

Having a role the first two years I attended gave me a purpose at the event. I was able to meet all the other volunteers as well. I went quickly from attending "on my own" to knowing people to invite to lunch.

JOIN THE HOST COMMITTEE

Is a major conference coming to your state? Get involved early in the planning for next year and help get the word out to your community. There are many ways a host committee can formally create a welcoming event. Designing materials for attendees visiting from afar and staffing a table where they answer questions about the local area are just two examples.

With "host committee" on your name tag, you are well positioned to say hello to everyone and anyone. While this may be your first time attending, you likely know quite a bit about the conference schedule and can be a great resource for other first-time attendees.

RAISE YOUR HAND

I've got a tip for people who are a bit shyer. During the breakout session Q&A, the dialogue usually moves very fast and the more outgoing people tend to dominate the conversation. Maybe you're not the type to just jump right in and tend to think through what you'd like to say before saying it. So by the time you're ready to speak up the conversation has moved on.

Raise your hand anyway. When you get called on, say, "A moment ago we were talking about XYZ." Then share your point or question. And add, "I would love to chat with anyone who is thinking about these issues. Find me at the end of this session." Then stick around at the end of the session and avoid jumping on your phone or otherwise looking busy.

Someone may come up to you right then, or a little while later during lunch, and start a conversation about the topic you raised. Since you're more comfortable in a one-on-one conversation, this is perfect for you. But it's only possible if you share what you are interested in talking about—you need to raise your hand.

HOST AN AFFINITY SESSION
Some conferences offer the opportunity to host an affinity session, a gathering space for people who share a common identity or geography. It can be especially useful at national conferences to host an affinity session for your region. Those who attend will be able to connect with people who live in their area, which will foster collaboration after the event.

You also could organize around a particular interest, which is what former CEO of Southwest Air and professional speaker, Howard Putnam, did. When he was first starting out in the speaking business, he got advice from Zig Ziglar. Zig, who was an influential author and motivational speaker, told Howard to join the National Speakers Association and get actively involved.

Howard has been connected to aviation his entire life. First learning how to fly out of the fields on his family's farm, he started his career as a baggage handler and worked his way to the top of the aviation industry. So it's an understatement to say aviation is an important part of his life.

"I had an idea to bring together professional speakers who have aviation in their background. Either they were a pilot, they were in the military, they love aviation, or their dad was a pilot. We were going to be inclusive and not exclusive. That's how Speaking Eagles was formed," said Howard.[5]

Speaking Eagles meets annually at the National Speakers Association conference, and they stay connected throughout the year through an active email list and website. Howard said, "That's how to do networking. Form little groups, reach out to others, and see if you have a common interest."[6]

At the same conference, there is a community group for podcast hosts and also a gathering for authors and those who are prioritizing writing their first book.

Any of these ideas could start out very informal. Reserve space at a nearby restaurant or tell people to meet you in the hotel lobby. Share the details through word of mouth and facilitate a conversation with whoever shows up. You can be more purposeful about who you want to invite and have a few people confirmed even before the conference begins.

If an idea takes off, then you can ask for space at the conference and have the gathering listed in official conference materials. You would be doing a tremendous service by organizing something like this, as it creates a space for like-minded or like-identified people to gather. You may be recognized for your leadership and thanked for helping others make quality connections.

JOIN A PANEL

Panelists often connect with each other before the conference to coordinate their sections of the program and of course get to know each other by speaking together on the panel. Sharing your experience and knowledge on a panel will lead attendees to recognize you as an expert in your field.

If you have an idea for a breakout session with a panel you can propose it. But there are ways to get invited to join a panel someone else coordinates.

If you enjoy a panel session, make an effort to meet the panelists after. Keep in touch with the person who coordinated the session and make it clear you have experience you would be willing to share. Reach out when you see the call for proposals and ask if they are putting together a panel again this year. Offer to set up a time to chat with them to see if you'd be a good fit as a panelist or could provide support in some other way. You could, for instance, help design the resource list given to attendees.

PRESENT A SESSION

While presenting requires some planning, as you'll need to have a presentation in mind before the application deadline, which is several months before the conference —it is definitely worth the time and effort. Standing in front of a room will make you more memorable, and after you present, people will reach out to speak with you about your work.

USE YOUR TIME WISELY

A quick note about pacing yourself at the conference; you can't go, go, go from morning to night and be at your best. Even my fellow extroverts will need time to reflect on what they've learned, synthesize the takeaways, and make a plan to put some of them into practice.

THREE THINGS A DAY

Choose three things a day you've identified as important or interesting to attend. Prioritize these three things when making decisions on how to spend your day.

One of the three should be entirely for you—something to truly feed you, something you really want to learn about or explore. This could be a workshop session not on your "should attend" list for work or a social event where you know you'll reconnect with old friends.

Once you have your three things a day, commit to them. For everything else, vote with your feet. If a session isn't meeting your needs go to a different one. If nothing else seems interesting, go to the hotel lobby to see who's available for a chat. I've found myself in wonderful conversations this way and learned things I could put into practice when I got home. Learning doesn't exist just within the breakout sessions. Your colleagues are incredibly resource-rich and knowledgeable.

If you're an introvert, you will likely want to schedule in some downtime in your room so you don't burn yourself out after just one day.

Stay on Track

If you are attending a conference with thousands or even tens of thousands of attendees, it may be helpful to think of the event not as one mega-event, but as several concurrent events.

Look through the program and you will notice sessions are divided up into different tracks. Focus your energy within just one or two of these tracks instead of going to lots of sessions across a wider spectrum of your interests.

This will help you hone in on a few quality connections. By choosing topics within just one or two tracks, you will increase the chance of attending sessions with some of the same people.

Make an effort to say hello the second or third time you spot someone from an earlier session, as they definitely have a lot in common with you.

Conferences and conventions with ten thousand plus attendees take some pre-planning, but the same steps you take to plan for a two-thousand-person event will help you navigate a much larger one.

Remember, if you arrive without a plan and just float from session to session, you might leave wondering whether it was worth your time and money.

THE ABCs OF BUSINESS CARDS

Always. Bring. Cards.

Even in the age of smartphones and apps, business cards are a critical tool for networking. This section is titled "The ABCs of Business Cards" because I believe you should Always. Bring. Cards. Remember those ABCs and you'll be ready to make great connections.

Here are just a few reasons to be sure you remember to pack yours:

BE MEMORABLE

A well-branded business card will make you more memorable. Point out something on your card as you're handing it over, encouraging the person you are speaking with to look at it. This will make it easier for them to recall your conversation when they see your card a few days later.

PHYSICAL REMINDER

When you receive or share a business card, it acts as a physical reminder of your conversation and any follow up you hope will happen.

This won't happen if you write yourself a note in your phone, send yourself an email, or use an app to exchange contact cards.

Helpful Notes

Before passing your card, jot a note on the back about what you talked about or the resource you hope they'll remember to share when they get back to the office.

Do the same when you receive a card—and also add the date and name of the event. This will increase the odds of doing the follow-up you said you'd do.

Avoid the Trash

After you get home, it's unlikely you empty your pockets and toss all the business cards you received into the recycling bin without a second glance. If someone hands you a cocktail napkin or a scrap of paper with their contact information on it, there is a higher probability it will be tossed it into the trash, maybe even before you get home, because it doesn't look important enough to keep.

Don't let this happen to your contact information when you are trying to stay connected.

Don't Have a Business Card?

If you don't have business cards, make an effort to get them before attending your next conference. Whether you are a newly promoted corporate executive, front-line staff at a nonprofit, or just launched your own business, you will benefit from having cards when you are at conferences and other networking events. This will allow you to easily exchange information with your peers and come home with new ideas and new connections in your field. Business cards may be ordered for less than twenty dollars from a site like Vistaprint.com.

When you are looking to change careers, it may not be appropriate or helpful to hand out a business card from your current company. You might want to have inquiries go to a different email address or brand yourself in an entirely different way.

Even if you are not job-hunting, you might find yourself looking for scraps of paper to share information about your side project. If this happens frequently, it is time for you to design a business card for the side project.

If you're between jobs and you're actively looking, I encourage you to design a card. You might be wondering what you would put on this card since you don't have a title. I've coached clients to put an aspirational title on their card as this leads to more meaningful conversations at conferences and other networking events.

If you are in college or grad school, you could put the year you graduate and your anticipated degree. To make your card more memorable, add a brief line about your career aspirations or an inspirational quote. This is more like a calling card than a business card but will keep you from hunting for scraps of paper when you make a solid connection.

This is not a major investment, so feel free to create a few different cards. If you are designing your own cards, please visit the "Resources" section for tips on content to include.

BENEFITS OF POCKETS

At a large conference, you're likely going to receive lots of business cards. Accept them from everyone who offers, but keep track of the ones to prioritize. One way to do this is to turn down a corner on those cards and write notes on the back of them. Place these priority business cards in a separate pocket to distinguish them easily from the larger stack of cards handed to you without an in-depth conversation.

WHAT IF YOU DON'T HAVE POCKETS?
Clothing designed for men will have not one, but multiple pockets. This makes it easier to keep track of the business cards received and to quickly reach the ones you are handing out.

Despite the growing popularity of ginormous-sized smartphones, women's professional clothing often has "for show only" pockets which only fit ChapStick®, if it has pockets at all. If you wear business and formal attire designed for women you will need to plan ahead when attending conferences and other networking events.

> **Women have had the right to vote since 1920. Why weren't pockets next on the agenda?**
>
> **A revolution is long overdue.**

POCKET ALTERNATIVES

I've met women who sew pockets into the inside of their jackets or sew on their own, larger, pockets into their dress pants—this is brilliant.

Short of sewing in pockets, planning ahead is key. Without any pre-planning, you might spend a few awkward minutes rooting around looking for a business card—one not horribly creased or smudged by whatever is floating at the bottom of your bag—in front of a virtual stranger you're trying to impress.

"Here, hold this..." a woman once said to me while digging deep into the cavernous vessel she had strapped to her shoulder.

Think for a moment about what is hiding in your bag, keeping you from quickly uncovering your business cards, and whether you want to share those contents with whomever you are networking.

Within Easy Reach

Of course, all of this presumes the bag is with you as you are mingling, and not tucked with your coat across the room. What are the chances your new connection will be waiting for you to return after you've dashed across a crowded room to retrieve a business card from your bag?

This is a common occurrence and is not limited to women. Everyone should realize the difference between having a business card, remembering to bring it to the event, and having it easily accessible while chatting.

Personally, I keep my business card holder in my back right pocket so I can easily hand out cards while holding a beverage in my left hand. Despite having multiple business cards for different projects, I'm able to give out the correct one without putting down my drink. My tip is to not over stuff the business card holder and before the event check to see if the cards are loose enough to be pulled out with ease.

Plan Ahead

If your outfit doesn't have adequate pockets, wear a jacket or sweater with a small business-card sized pocket for the cards you give out and a place for you to tuck the cards you receive. You may find wearing a jacket or sweater helps in other ways since most breakout rooms are over-air-conditioned.

Designate a small leather purse as your go-to bag for networking events—so you know you'll always have your essentials with you. If you always bring the same purse, it takes the guesswork out of packing.

Wherever you keep your business cards, put them in a business card holder to help prevent cards from getting stray ink marks from pens, smudges from makeup, or folds from being crushed.

The exception to using a business card holder is when you are able to put a few business cards in your name badge. Do this so you always have a card with you, even if you leave your jacket and bag at the table while on the buffet line.

DRESS CODE CONUNDRUM

While we're on the topic of what to wear, I wanted to address a question I've been asked by some of the women I coach. How do you figure out the "dress code" for conferences? I think we can agree, women have a tougher time figuring out the "dress code" than men. For men, the choice is often which suit to wear and no further worry. Of course, there is a limit to the adage "overdressing is better than under dressing." Wearing an evening gown might draw negative attention if everyone else is in business attire.

There are a few things to keep in mind as you put together your wardrobe for the event. For starters, be kind to your feet—you will be walking and standing more than usual. This isn't the right time to break in a new pair of shoes or wear those great looking shoes which make your feet ache.

Select clothing you will not need to keep readjusting and will resist wrinkling after several hours of sitting. Add in a pop of color, French blue or another bright color will help you stand out in a sea of gray and black suits. Before packing, look at photos from last year's event for guidance on what the range has been.

BE EFFECTIVE

STRATEGY ONLY GETS YOU SO FAR

Strategy will only get you so far. You can have the perfect outfit, researched who you wanted to meet, business cards within easy reach, and even drafted your follow-up email, but it will be all for nothing if you aren't effective while at the conference. Being effective is about having a strong sense of purpose, the skills to meet your goals, and a commitment to follow-through. This section covers a range of topics to help you make the most of this conference experience and stories of ineffective networking illustrate what not to do.

ARE YOU A GUEST OR A HOST?

With some advance research, you are pretty confident you'll be able to make good connections at this conference. You walk in and... now what? How do you jump into conversations?

The first question to ask yourself is, "Am I a guest or a host?" If you're a regular and know many people at the event, then consider yourself a host. This is true more times than you might have realized. Being a host means you go out of your way to welcome others and make introductions. You look for outliers and help them feel connected. Instead of scattershot attendance, focus your energy on just a few organizations' events to quickly become a regular. In the next section, "Be Inclusive," I'll cover some of the benefits to being a regular and having a host mentality.

Your First Time

Of course, there's always a first time when you're a newcomer. What do you do if you are a guest? We have all experienced this moment: standing in a hall full of people we don't know and not knowing where to go.

If you are an introvert and/or shy and you find networking very stressful, you may naturally gravitate to the edges of the room. However, this can be counterproductive to making connections.

Yes, you may find it's easier to meet other wallflowers, and it might be a great conversation, but what are your options at the end of the conversation? If neither of you knows other people in the room, then you can't get introduced or make introductions. This makes exiting the conversation more difficult and potentially awkward. "Really great to meet you. Excuse me, I need to find the restroom." Their reply, "Oh, thanks, I'll follow you." Awkward.

Mingle in the middle of the room.

LOOK FOR THE CROISSANT

Start by circling the room to get the lay of the land. Pay attention to people's body language, and scan for openings in groups of three or four attendees who are having a casual conversation (avoid interrupting duos in a dynamic conversation). Become aware of who is more open to chatting by observing the body language of those around you.

I share more details about my "croissants vs. bagels" concept in the "Be Inclusive" section.

GET IN LINE

If you've completed your lap around the room and didn't see a conversation opening, then get in line for food or a drink. As you're moving through the line, make eye contact with someone near you and start a casual conversation. You could ask them their opinion about the specialty drink they ordered or comment on how delicious the buffalo cheese dip is. The point is to keep it casual—this is not the moment to whip out your card and pitch them.

It's important to keep these interactions upbeat and resist the temptation to connect through complaining. While it's common to complain about the weather, traffic, sports, politics, or the stock market, these are not great opening lines, as they tend to result in rote replies. If done in excess, you will be pegged as a downer, and no one wants to hang out with a complainer. Instead, use this as an opportunity to make a positive observation or ask a question about the food or drink in front of you— just something small to get a conversation started with someone standing near you.

You'll find it's much easier to meet people when they are not standing with their circle of friends. This is more likely to happen when they are in line for food or a drink. This is also a key difference between networking events and conferences versus any night of the week at a bar. While it's possible to apply these tips in any social situation, people are looking to make connections at a networking event. So meeting someone casually while getting a drink may lead to you being invited to meet the colleague they came with, who is in a conversation with a couple of people they just met. Now, instead of not knowing a single soul in the room, you are interacting with four people who are all there to get to know new people!

Avoid Corners

Don't take breaks in corners; go outside or into a bathroom stall instead. If you stand in the corner, an outgoing extrovert may come and speak to you. In their excitement to share a story, they may be a bit obtuse and not notice your lack of interest or your desire to wrap up the conversation. If this happens you may feel trapped and have no easy way to gracefully exit, since your egress is through the oblivious person speaking to you who is not noticing your subtle hints.

It is best to mingle in the middle of the room and look for conversation openings.

STARTING A CONVERSATION

You now have some ideas for how to approach people at conferences and might be wondering what you say to start a conversation.

WORST OPENING LINE

Picture this: You're at a crowded event and spot a familiar face, but you can't quite place why you know them. You maneuver a little closer so you're able to read their name tag. You now know the person's name, but you can't remember how you know them.

You start asking yourself questions to see if you can jog your memory:

Was his name on the recent donations list I just read?

Did I read his name in the paper this morning?

Is he getting an award tonight?

After a few minutes of being lost in thought, you look up and can no longer spot this person. They've moved to another part of the event and you're now standing in a crowded room by yourself with a strong sense you should have said hello.

What I just described is the worst opening line, when it doesn't even happen. In this scenario, if you do figure out what you would have spoken about with this person and write them an email after the event, this is not actually a follow-up message. It is just email, and you don't have to leave the house to send email.

If you are going to go through the effort to leave your house, get nicely dressed and all made up, and find your way to the event, make sure people know you were there (and not just because you checked in on Facebook).

Best Opening Line

Here's a different take on the same situation: You're at a crowded event and spot a familiar face, but you can't quite place why you know them. Despite moving closer and reading their name tag, you still can't remember whether you're thanking them, congratulating them, or anything else you should be saying when you meet them.

You catch their eye as you pass them, turn, and say, "Hi, my name is _____. I'm on the board." They respond with their name and affiliation, and you say, "Nice to meet you. How did you hear about tonight?" or "Nice to meet you. What are you looking forward to tonight?" Now you two are in a conversation and when you go home tonight you can send them a follow-up message.

If you struggle with your opening line to the point where you don't say anything, you are missing opportunities to connect. Keep your opening line simple. My preferred opening line is, "Hi, my name is _____," followed by any relevant affiliations. By not over thinking this you are more likely to approach people who seem familiar or anyone who happens to catch your eye. Keep in mind you aren't going to follow this up by pitching them. Save your sales pitch for when you've already confirmed they are interested in what you are offering.

THREE SECONDS

Yes, it can be a bit daunting to go talk to people you don't know, but don't hesitate more than three seconds before going over to them. Three seconds is all you get to be nervous. Any longer and you'll talk yourself out of going over at all.

Remember to keep it simple: "Hi, my name is..."

ASK OPEN-ENDED QUESTIONS

Once you've introduced yourself, focus on open-ended questions to invite them to bring more of themselves into the room rather than zeroing in on what's on their business card.

The question could be related to the conference:

"What drew you to this session?" "What's been the highlight of your day so far?" "Learn anything you know you'll be able to use when you get home?" Or even simply, "How did you hear about this event?"

Or it could be a question inviting them to talk about something they care about:

"Have any travel plans you're looking forward to?" "If you had free time, how would you fill it?" This can be a great way to get them talking about a personal passion project.

Or, "What do you do when you aren't (whatever topic brought you two together)?" (e.g., "What do you do when you aren't talking about finances?")

You can follow this last question with one more directly related to work, such as, "Does that help in some way with what you do for work?" or you can say, "Sounds like a great way to get outside the world of (the work you have in common)."

If they are clearly a long-time attendee (lots of ribbons on their name tag) you could ask what keeps them coming back each year or what has been their best takeaway. Any of these questions will allow you to dig a little deeper and through conversation find out more about each other.

Be prepared to answer the same open-ended questions you ask, as there is a high likelihood they will answer and then reframe the question for you to answer it as well.

> ### "To be interesting, be interested."
> ### —Dale Carnegie[7]

LEAVE THEM THINKING YOU'RE FASCINATING

When someone is speaking, listen intently and ask thoughtful questions to engage them further. Don't have any knowledge about the topic they brought up? Not sure how to respond? Keep the conversation going by saying, "Really. That's so interesting. Tell me more." This roughly translates to, "I have no idea what to say right now." but won't stop the conversation in its tracks.

Is the conversation not coming around to something you're really interested in discussing? Wrap up the conversation a few minutes later. Don't drag it out. The person you were just talking to will walk away thinking you're fascinating.

Seriously. All you said was your name. You didn't tell your whole life story or a long and involved sales pitch.

You asked thoughtful questions which helped them show up more in the room. They were able to share a bit more about themselves and one of their passions. Later, when they see you approach their circle of friends, they'll instinctively create space for you to join their group. They don't know a lot about you, but they do know you made them feel welcomed and interesting, so they will be open to reconnecting.

Beware of Navel Gazing

Always greet people by saying your name; don't assume they remember. Even at a conference when you are wearing a name tag, this is a good idea. Too often, name tags at conferences are hovering closer to one's navel than their lapel. So during the "networking luncheon" everyone's name tag is hanging below the table. During the networking break in the hall, you need to look down at someone's navel while shaking their hands—making it harder to bluff that you remembered their name all along. While convenient, because they work with any outfit, lanyards are the cause of all this navel gazing. Tie up some of the lanyard to lift your name tag higher.

Nix "What Do You Do?"

It's a tired line, and if it's one of the first things you ask it can feel like a screening process. Instead, find something you are both excited to talk about, such as travel, and the conversation will go deeper and may lead to a longer lasting connection.

The chances of you walking into a room and selling something to someone you just met are very, very low.

People buy from people they know, like, and trust.

A thirty-second pitch does not build trust. So take the time to get to know the people you meet, ask them questions, and show genuine interest in their responses.

Remember in the "Be Strategic" section, I suggested you prep an answer to this ubiquitous question. Rather than saying your job title and company, answer using this syntax: "I help ___ do ___." Another example is, "I inspire ___ to do ___."

Hopefully, you've done this prep work and now have a new way of answering this question and also a couple of quick stories to illustrate your work and its impact in the world. Replying in this new way can be especially useful if the answer you used to give caused people's eyes to glaze over. Don't get screened out because of your job title; create opportunities for people to connect to you and your work.

Awkward Opening Lines

All questions are not equal, and some have the opposite effect of making someone feel welcomed and connected to you. When you first meet someone, avoid calling out difference. This could result in them feeling alienated or like they don't belong. We do this more often than we might realize.

To learn best practices on what NOT to say when greeting someone, read about "The Downside to Being a Unicorn" in the "Be Inclusive" section.

SMALL NETWORKING MOMENTS

Picture this: It's early in the morning, and you're on your way to a local conference; or it's late at night, and you're flying to a conference across the country. Knowing you would be out of the office at least one day, you stayed late several days in the last week to get work done. In fact, you're still thinking about a project at work and wondering how you'll meet the deadline while being out of the office.

The last thing on your mind is networking.

Ideally, you'd have thought through a strategic networking plan before going to the conference, but even without one, you can take advantage of all the small networking moments throughout the day. One example is the opportunity to meet fellow attendees at breakout sessions.

Does this scene sound familiar? You don't know many people at the conference, and you don't enjoy mingling during the breaks, so you go directly to the breakout session room five to ten minutes before the program begins.

You choose a chair as far apart as possible from everyone else in the room, taking the aisle seat in the last row if it's still available. Then, quickly get on your phone to check work emails, scroll through Facebook, or play Bejeweled.

As the room fills up a few people are sitting near you— perhaps even one seat over. The room is less than half filled and almost entirely silent. You and almost everyone else is focusing on their phones.

Even if you are not the most gregarious person, you can take advantage of these small networking moments. After all, the people around you chose the same session as you AND ducked into the session early to avoid the chaos in the hallway, so you likely have something in common with them.

You will have a much better opportunity for a great connection meeting attendees in this room, compared to meeting someone randomly in line at the Starbucks in the hotel lobby.

Here with colleagues? Go mingle.
Here alone? Don't stay that way.

When I work with conference planners, I recommend they establish a conference ethos, "Here with colleagues? Go mingle. Here alone? Don't stay that way."

Have this phrase on the projector screen as attendees enter breakout sessions and on a signboard at the ballroom entrance. It is as a good reminder you can catch up with your co-workers at home; at the conference, take advantage of the opportunities around you.

When this becomes the ethos of the conference, the idea of joining a table of strangers for lunch won't feel quite as uncomfortable even to someone who is shy.

SEVEN TIPS FOR CONFERENCE BREAKOUTS

Worried no one will talk to you? Use these seven tips to take advantage of small networking moments and meet like-minded colleagues.

Don't Sit Right Away

Here's what I do when I get to a breakout session. I put my bag down next to someone and while standing turn to the person sitting closest to me and say, "Good morning," or, "Hi, my name is..." Usually, the person sitting near us looks over because this was a shift in what had been a silent room. I say hello to the other person and ask if the two of them have met yet. They obviously haven't, but now realize they should.

Ask Relevant Questions

"What drew you to this session?" is a good conversation starter, but you can get much more specific. Think about why you selected this session and turn it into a question: "I'd like to learn the latest techniques for (topic). What has been your experience with (blank)?"

You can also ask a general question, such as, "How has the conference been so far?" or "What has been your favorite session so far?"

Look for Outliers

Are you more outgoing? Move around the room while you are waiting for the session to begin, and start a conversation with people sitting off by themselves. Gentle humor about how we're all so quick to get on our phones (evidenced by five people sitting within arm's length of each other in silence on their phones) is a good ice-breaker if followed by a question or two to get the conversation started. Since the program starting will eventually interrupt your conversation, this isn't risky in the same way it would be to speak to a wallflower in the hallway. There will be a natural end to your conversation.

It's possible someone is concentrating on a work project and they don't want to be disturbed. Don't be deterred by one person; the rest of the room is likely more receptive, as they realize meeting people is a big reason why they are at the conference in the first place.

MEET THE PRESENTER

Excuse yourself to say hello to the presenter after you've helped a few people engage in conversation.

As the room fills up, the presenter has likely finished finagling with their PowerPoint slides and is waiting expectantly at the front of the room. This is a great opportunity for you to chat with them before they speak. You don't have to prepare a speech; simply say what you are looking forward to about their presentation.

If you've ever presented, you know how nice it is when someone comes up to speak to you before your talk to say how much they are looking forward to it. The presenter may be looking for a workshop example and what you share leads them to ask to use your question as an example later in the session. This is great because you'll get a lot of advice from the group and the people in this session will know who you are to follow up with you later in the conference.

Of course, if the presenter is still fiddling with their PowerPoint trying to get it to look something other than all green, then you'll need to give them some space. But most times, the presenter is ready to go and just waiting for the room to fill up. Since you've done a bit of research beforehand, you know something about the presenter so you can have a quick conversation which might be memorable to them.

Plan to send a follow-up note; mention it was great meeting them and thank them for their presentation. If the information the presenter provided was especially helpful for your work, you might want to invite them to meet up during the conference. This could be for coffee or just a quick chat in the hallway before lunch.

The goal is to have a moment or two with whoever is speaking before they get on stage and everyone else knows who they are. At the end of the session, everyone will queue up to meet the presenter, which brings me to my next tip...

Work the Line

At the end of the session a few people will form a line to speak to the presenter. Out of all the people you might want to meet "spontaneously" at the conference, these people have also selected a session you are interested in and enjoyed it enough to stay after to meet the presenter. This is a great opportunity for you to meet someone with shared interests. Stand off to the side of the end of the line and ask an open-ended question about the presentation. For example, "Those were great examples. Has anyone found a similar outcome when you tried it at your organization?" An outgoing extrovert will respond, and a moment later you'll be in a conversation with a few of the people who had been waiting quietly in line.

Why do this? There is a networking opportunity after every breakout. It could be fifteen minutes in the hallway between sessions, lunch, or an evening reception.

Leave in Pairs

Rather than walk out of this breakout session on your own and have to figure out who to speak with once in the hallway, wouldn't it be better to walk out with someone who just attended the same session as you and liked it enough to stay after to speak with the presenter? Then you won't have to navigate the coffee break on your own, and you might be introduced to your new contact's colleagues or invited to join them for lunch.

Paying attention to small networking moments like this will help you meet the kind of people you want to know:

attendees with the same interests as you and a willingness to engage.

NETWORK ANYWHERE

For those who are a bit savvier with their networking skills, saying hello and asking an open-ended question also works when you're in line at the hotel's Starbucks.

I did this at a convention and ended up having breakfast with the CEO of a multi-million-dollar company. He is an introvert, so we wouldn't have likely connected if I hadn't said hello first. We crossed paths several more times throughout the convention. He was also a guest on my podcast!

You never know unless you say hello.

BEYOND BREAKOUT SESSIONS AND THE HALLWAY

Networking should not be limited to breakout sessions and the hallway. At breakfast and lunch breaks you'll have an opportunity to meet attendees, but only if you are mindful and don't gravitate to sitting with the colleagues you see all the time. This limits your ability to make new connections.

Remember: "Here with colleagues? Go mingle. Here alone? Don't stay that way."

People from the same organization often sit together whenever possible. This reduces the possibility they will meet their peers from different organizations. This happens all the time. You've probably seen it even within your own organization when departments attend an all-staff training and sit with colleagues from their own department, missing the opportunity to get to know other colleagues from outside their department.

ABOUT THOSE NAME TAGS

Name tags are only useful if you can easily read them. If you are wearing a lanyard, your name tag is likely hanging below the table's edge during lunch. Remember my tip: tie up some of the lanyard to lift your name tag higher to make your name visible. This will make it easier for other attendees to remember your name, as they can read your name tag after you introduce yourself.

BE A HOST

In the "Be Inclusive" section of this book, I share tips on how to host a table at lunch. This is an excellent way to meet people and saves you from wandering around looking for a table to join.

DON'T DO THIS

One of the reasons you may be reluctant to network at conferences is because you've been on the receiving end of some terrible networking practices.

Sometimes the best way to recognize your own bad networking techniques is to see them in someone else. In 2006, I founded a social justice Meetup in Boston, called Socializing for Justice; I was relentless about giving out the group's business card to help grow our membership.

I enthusiastically gave one to everyone I met, often before they had an opportunity to ask me questions about the group. I was eager to spread the word about this great new resource and wasn't aware I could be coming off as pushy.

THE YOGA INSTRUCTOR
Toward the end of the year, I attended a networking event and briefly met a yoga instructor. Actually, "met" is too strong a word for our interaction. She was holding her business cards out in front of her, slightly fanned, and with the flick of the wrist was handing them to everyone who came within reach. I was not in the market for a yoga instructor, but I dutifully made an attempt to engage her in a conversation to see if we might have other interests in common. She looked over my shoulder

throughout our brief conversation, and was more interested in handing out her cards than chatting. I wrapped up the conversation within moments and moved on.

One year later, I met this same yoga instructor at a networking event. This time she was standing next to another young woman—both posed with their cards fanned out before them. I said hello as I was walking by, and she quickly handed me her card saying, "This is my new card. And (while reaching for her friend's card) this is the photographer who took my photo for it." I accepted the two cards and kept walking, as I already knew she had no real interest in engaging further.

Her actions puzzled me, as I had already begun to rethink my own quick-draw approach to networking. I had learned I was much more effective if I took the time to find out how I could help the person I was talking to and then mention a resource my organization provided. Her "spray and pray" method had been a real turn-off and drove home for me how important quality was over quantity when networking.

STOP SPRAYING AND PRAYING
Whether you know the phrase "spray and pray" or not, you probably have experienced this phenomenon, and possibly, like me, you have been guilty of doing it. It took me a while to realize this wasn't the most effective

way to network. When friends and colleagues began to talk up my organization, instead of me doing all the promotion, membership started to grow exponentially.

Stephanie Chung, a speaker and coach who is known as "The High-Ticket Sales Closer," knows how important relationship building is to selling. Which is why she said, "I hate when people spam me. What that means is you come up and shove your business card at me and start rattling off all this stuff that you do, you haven't asked me a question, and don't know if I need what you have to offer. It's so insulting. I hate it."[8]

This is definitely the wrong way to try to connect. When people tell me they don't like networking, it's this kind of behavior that is turning them off.

As Stephanie said, "There is a protocol and an etiquette to how to do it correctly. I do spend a lot of time making sure that I'm building that relationship. If it was worth having the conversation and worth exchanging the cards, then I'm going to now be diligent and make sure I'm constantly cultivating that relationship."[9]

Having the right mindset is critical. Stephanie said, "It's always me coming to them from a service perspective. 'Hey, how can I help you?' 'Hey, there's someone I thought you'd want to meet...' I'm always giving, giving, giving. Because I know somewhere along the line the law of reciprocity will kick in and they will want to give in return."[10]

THE SALESMAN

I remember being at a networking dinner and the guy next to me handed me a stack of his business cards and said, "Take one and pass them around the table." I politely returned the stack of cards and suggested he chat with other guests about his job first. He could have moved to an empty chair on the other end of the table to initiate conversation with guests sitting further away.

I then asked about his job—he was a salesman who had just started at a new job. Our brief conversation was interrupted as a new guest arrived and was approaching us to say hello and introduce herself. After a brief handshake, she turned to walk away, and the salesman quickly handed her his business card and said his ten-second sales pitch. Someone across the table mentioned she was not his target demographic—which he could have discovered if he had spoken with her for even a moment or two.

This scenario, with different characters, repeats itself at networking events and conferences all over the world.

> Business cards are communication devices.

What are your business cards saying about you and your business when you're spraying them all around the room and praying someone will respond?

CHAMBER CULTURE

I witnessed this at a chamber of commerce event. Before taking my seat, I was chatting with a chamber member, and after a few minutes, we exchanged business cards. Seeing this, someone interrupted us to mention we'd all be exchanging business cards when we sat down.

Wait, what? I shouldn't exchange cards now while having a conversation because business cards will be dealt out like a deck of cards once we are all seated?

After we had sat down, each attendee stood for thirty to sixty seconds and gave their pitch. As promised, a stack of their business cards was passed around the table. The problem was, by the time I received each person's stack, they weren't speaking anymore, and I wasn't able to easily track who I wanted to follow up with or what each member had shared. It felt incredibly ineffective.

> **People do business with
> people they know, like, and trust.**
>
> **That trust isn't based on a
> thirty-second sales pitch.**

Small Business Expo

We have a lot of work to do to flip the usual networking strategy and make the focus building relationships, instead of simply collecting business cards.

This was the thought I had when I came across an enormous business card display at a small business expo—racks and racks of business cards propped up on easels. Altogether there were small stacks of business cards from well over one hundred attendees.

I watched as two business owners went through the entire display at the end of the event, taking one card from each small stack. Curious, I asked these business owners what they planned to do with all of these cards. The answer seemed obvious once they replied: They were adding all of these business cards to their mailing list.

Really. This was their plan. And in some ways it was genius—I mean, if you think the goal of networking is to collect business cards, why bother taking the time to talk to people?

> This is not relationship building,
> this is business card collecting.

The Real Estate Professional

At a different networking event, a real estate professional started a conversation by handing me his business card. He then pitched me his services, and I explained I wasn't looking to buy or sell a home. When our conversation wrapped up a few minutes later, I didn't offer him a business card. He loitered nearby while I was speaking to someone else, and when there was a slight lull in my conversation he jumped in and said, "May I have your card?"

Reluctantly I handed it to him, as I knew I was about to be added to his mailing list. Which, indeed is what happened. He followed up right away with a poorly formatted mail-merged email template, which made no attempt to seem personal. Despite not responding, he added me to his email list and continued to send me emails I had zero interest in receiving.

After several months of this, I finally wrote him to remind him I had not asked to be added to his email list and, in fact, had not been interested in his services. Ironically, we met at a networking training; yet this real estate professional did what he had always done—he seemed to learn nothing from the training. If I ever need someone to help me buy or sell a home, this is not someone I would give my business.

What I just described has happened so many times with so many different real estate professionals, I can now spot them from a mile away. They are working the room, moving among guests looking for a mark, engaging just long enough to see if someone is a client prospect and then moving on.

In defense of the real estate profession, I have also met agents who are quite engaging and lovely to chat with at events. They focus on offering value first and don't ever pressure someone upon meeting them for the first time. When I meet those types of agents, I pass along an idea shared with me by a real estate agent many years ago.

At closing, this agent would share a list of five charities in their area and ask the homeowners to designate which he should send one hundred dollars in the new home-owner's name. This lets the new homeowner know about charities in their new neighborhood, and the charity they select has a new contact to add to their database. I thought this was brilliant and a way to differentiate their real estate services. I have been happy to share this idea with any real estate professional who didn't focus on pitching me the first time we met.

Who do you think I'll reach out to when I need a real estate agent? The agents who shoved their cards at me or the agents whom I've stayed in touch with through mutual interests and overlapping social networks?

"Spraying and praying" is a waste of time and does not build strong relationships which will help you meet your professional and business goals.

Two Ears and One Mouth

> "We have two ears and one mouth so we can listen twice as much as we speak."
>
> —Epictetus (AD 55–c.135)

Talking more than listening is not a new phenomenon. Nowadays, there are so many ways to communicate, but we don't seem much better at communication. Quite the opposite is true in our fast-paced world.

Take note of how much you speak when you are at your next networking event. Sometimes we talk too much when meeting new people because we're nervous and want to fill any awkward pauses.

The pause may not be awkward for the person we are speaking with, but we perceive it to be. Rather than overwhelm someone with endless chatter, check for signs they are interested. Or better yet, stop talking about yourself and ask questions.

Don't Be a Shark

Don't be one of those completely overbearing people who push their own agendas, but do not show genuine interest in the people they meet. Those people come across as sharks, circling the event looking for the next person they will take down with their endless blather and self-importance.

Most people long to be listened to, so it's possible once someone feels comfortable sharing with you, you won't be able to share a lot about yourself.

Remember what I said earlier, it's possible to ask lots of questions, share very little about yourself, and leave them thinking you're fascinating.

Don't Be Bait Either

It's going to happen. A "serial networker" will approach you who isn't very good at switching from their pitch to a mutually beneficial conversation. Try to get beyond the pitch by asking about other topics or commenting on what is going on in the room. If the conversation keeps coming back to their pitch, it is best to recognize what is happening and wrap up the conversation.

Are You the Whale?

If you are more advanced in your career, you may attract people who are hoping to receive some assistance from you to help them advance in their career. You may have people ask, "How can I help you?" and then feel trapped into responding in kind even though you have no specific request for them.

You should not feel trapped into offering assistance. Doing a favor under these circumstances won't result in a positive glow from helping someone, but instead a feeling of obligation.

Here is another way to respond:

"How kind of you to offer. Nothing comes to mind right now. My philosophy is to get to know someone for a while before asking for a favor. I hope we continue to cross paths and learn more about each other's work."

TEN IS BETTER THAN ONE HUNDRED

Expos, conventions, and conferences can be great places to build your professional network. With a strategic goal in mind and some pre-planning, you can meet people who want to hear more about whatever it is you're selling. Better to leave with just ten business cards after having meaningful conversations where you can offer value upfront than to go home with stacks of business cards from fleeting conversations or collected from the expo business card display.

Those ten contacts will remember you when you reach out to them after the event. Ideally you will build your initial introduction into an authentic relationship where you choose to stay in touch and happen to do business together now and again.

When this happens it doesn't feel like networking—because you're doing business with people you genuinely enjoy getting to know.

Remember, people do business with people they know, like, and trust. Adding people to your email list without their consent isn't going to win their trust or make them want to work with you.

QUALITY OVER QUANTITY

When I first moved to Boston in 2002, I was a regular at an open mic night. Other than getting up to make a community announcement, I never shared onstage. I was attending because I was new to the area and had found this to be a very welcoming community.

I kept coming back because I was starting to find friendships among the many attendees who also returned week after week.

The event organizer had a rule about flyering. Flyers and business cards could not be placed on the chairs before the event started. You could only hand these marketing materials out as attendees were leaving the event.

I asked why this rule existed. The event organizer told me it hadn't at first and piles of flyers and business cards had been placed on chairs before the event. At the end of the night, after the chairs were stacked, all of those pieces of paper still needed to be cleaned up from the floor.

When attendees first arrived, they were busy settling into the space and catching up with friends, so everything on their chair was swept onto the floor. Attendees were more motivated to pay attention to the flyers on their way out, after hearing the community announcements and becoming interested in one of the events or services being shared.

How does this relate to conferences? Don't bother getting to the luncheon or breakout session early to place your card on every seat. This isn't going to be effective. Focus instead on having meaningful conversations and look for opportunities to share your expertise. This could be during Q&A at the end of a breakout session or by hosting a pop-up session in the hallway during lunch.

Do This

You've now learned a variety of ways to meet people and start a conversation, and you've read examples of bad networking practices. What else do you need to head to your next conference with confidence?

An Upbeat Attitude

If you follow the steps in the "Be Strategic" section, you will have a strong sense of why you are attending this particular conference. Being aware of all the possible connections you could make at this event should help you get excited. If you show up without doing this pre-planning, you might be dreading going, which will have an impact on your attitude as you approach people.

If you can't get excited about this conference, if you aren't looking forward to what you'll learn and who you'll meet, then you may show up in a foul and angsty mood. Complaining about the weather, traffic, or menu selection is not a great way to start a conversation and will likely turn other attendees off from getting to know you. Opportunity awaits, so shake off your anxiety and get pumped!

Firm Handshake

> In this Facebook world, people
> have forgotten how to do face time.

Handshakes are important cues to mark the beginning and the end of a conversation. Later, I will share how handshakes, when used correctly, will help you wrap up and move on. Before I get into those details, let me first describe what a handshake is and isn't.

Too often, people will grip and rip. It's as if they're looking to win big with three 7s, but your arm is not a slot machine.

Remember, you want to leave an impression, but not a bruise.

At the other end of the spectrum are the people who don't give you their full hand when they shake, just their fingertips. Now, if you were the Queen of England you could get away with this, but you're not.

So what is a proper handshake? The web between your thumb and pointer finger touches the web of the other person's hand, you grip, and release. Feel the need to pump? Twice, not more. You don't want to come across as over-eager or pushy.

MINDFUL EYE CONTACT

Ever talk to someone who can't seem to stay focused on you or doesn't appear to be paying attention to what you are saying? They keep looking past you, scanning the crowd, checking their phone, watching the door—it's so distracting!

Hello? Are you at all interested in what I'm saying?

Since you've experienced this, you're probably aware of how important eye contact is to let the person you're talking to know you're present and engaged with them.

It's also a good indicator it's time to wrap up if you realize you can't maintain good eye contact.

If you notice your ex, the person you want to work for, or a friend you haven't seen in ages walk in the room, this is understandably distracting. Best to wrap up the conversation you're in and pick it up again at another point. Otherwise, you'll be conveying disinterest, which is off-putting.

There are other reasons you might not be able to stay focused on the conversation: you are hungry, tired, waiting for an important call, or worried about your parking meter running out.

It's important to be mindful and present if you want to connect with another person authentically. Unable to do this? Wrap up the conversation and move on.

For a variety of reasons, some people have a hard time maintaining eye contact. If this describes you, just know you'll have to compensate to be sure the person you are talking to knows you are present and interested in what they are saying.

BUSINESS CARDS WITHIN REACH

Gone are the days where you can get a book of matches from the bar to jot down your number. Why? Most places have banned smoking indoors, so bars no longer give out matchbooks.

Figure you'll just jot your info on a cocktail napkin? You're handing over something which looks like trash and will likely end up thrown away when they get home.

To make a strong first impression, have a business card handy.

Bring business cards when there's even the slightest chance of a networking opportunity. You may be surprised to find this means having them with you at all times since networking can happen anywhere. Be certain you have them within easy reach and not in your bag across the room.

Personally, I like to use three pockets when I'm networking. One for the business cards I'm giving out, one for the ones I want to be certain I keep track of, and one for the cards I received without any real conversation.

Have you experienced this? You're standing in one of those tight networking circles and someone hands out their business card to everyone. Suddenly, everyone starts passing out cards. It's like you're in a poker game.

Glance through those cards, but be sure the cards you receive after a great connection are easily identifiable when you get home. If those cards can be quickly pulled from the pile, it will make following up much easier.

As I mentioned in the "Be Strategic" section, women will have to plan ahead since professional clothing designed for women often has no pockets or pockets too small to fit a business cards holder.

PEN HANDY

Even though we all walk around with computers in the form of phones, there is still a need for pens now and again. It is particularly useful to have a pen to jot a note on a business card as you receive it—to remind yourself what you had agreed to follow up about after the event. You may also want to do the same for the business card you hand over—to remind them what you had discussed or what follow up they had agreed to do.

If you have pens with your logo and website on them, you might want to carry a few extras with you. Then, if someone asks to borrow a pen, you can tell them they can keep it, and it will be another reminder of your conversation.

ELEVATOR PITCH

In the "Be Strategic" section, we covered the importance of having a strategy and a sense of purpose. Your elevator pitch should be tweaked based on who you hope to meet and what you want to discuss. Keep it brief and be sure to pause to leave room for questions.

A common mistake is to say your elevator pitch right away, while still pumping someone's hand. At which point you don't know if the person you are meeting has any interest in what you are sharing. Start the conversation by introducing yourself and asking an open-ended question. Then, listen for clues which will connect this person's interests to what you are there to talk about. When there is an opening offer value, before you pitch.

ACTIVE LISTENING

I've already covered how important it is to maintain eye contact and not look past the person you are speaking to as others are coming in the door. You'll also want to show you are paying attention by repeating key points or asking clarifying questions.

Let's revisit what Dale Carnegie said, "To be interesting, be interested." Such a simple turn of phrase which holds such deep meaning.

While you want to have goals when you attend networking events, you don't want to meet your goals in such a way that you are turning people off. It's dangerous to focus solely on the metrics of the number of people you meet, losing sight of the ultimate goal—connection.

If someone you meet wants to stay connected and is willing to schedule a time to chat again when you reach out to them after the event, then you are doing something right. If you dutifully meet everyone in the room and send out an impersonal blast email, you should not be surprised if you get very few responses.

LEAVE ON A HIGH NOTE

Keep in mind you are not going to meet someone and immediately sell them something. Relationships are built over time, and that only happens if the person you're speaking with wants to connect with you again.

In fact, think about wrapping up the conversation while it's still in full swing, rather than waiting until it peters out. Your goal should be to leave the conversation on a high note, to make the person feel great about the interaction they had with you.

This way, even if you don't get the opportunity to make your pitch, this person will want to chat with you again at this conference and introduce you to their colleagues. By the end of the conference, you will have had several meaningful conversations and be much more memorable when you reach out after the event.

MAKE GENUINE CONNECTIONS

I organized the networking dinner I mentioned in the "Don't Do This" section. The same woman who received a business card with a ten-second pitch for services she didn't need ended up asking me about my work. We chatted for a few minutes about networking angst, and she learned I had a podcast about networking and leadership.

A moment later she asked if I had a business card. I handed one to her, but I resisted handing one to everyone else who might have overheard our conversation at the table. Before the dinner ended, the woman across from her asked me for my business card and had a specific idea of how we might work together.

Rather than putting one of my business cards at every place setting, I built credibility and trust by convening the networking dinner, making sure everyone felt welcome, and sharing a bit about my work without doing a heavy pitch—and it worked. Without pitching, first-time guests left with my business card and heard my work highly praised by a colleague.

Those relationships are still nascent and may not directly turn into business, but I don't host networking events with the goal of lining up business after one brief encounter. I host networking events throughout the month to broaden and deepen my professional network. Over time this will lead to new clients.

*Word of mouth praise is
still the best promotion.*

CLOSE THE LOOP

Closing the loop—letting the person who made an introduction know what transpired—is a crucial but often overlooked step in networking. Let's say you run into a colleague at the conference and share you have been trying to meet an influencer in your industry. The influencer isn't at this particular conference, but your colleague offers to reach out and see if the influencer would be open to this introduction when they get back to their office—then they actually remember to do this.

You will, of course, thank your colleague for making the introduction, but will you remember to follow up with them again? They will be left to wonder if the connection proved beneficial or not. I know, life gets busy and this step often gets lost in the shuffle, but over time you will erode the goodwill being offered by this colleague.

A simple email might suffice, but if the introduction landed you a great job or a five-figure client, then up your game and send a thank you package.

In the "Resources" section, I share detailed steps for writing an effective email introduction. This will be helpful when you are asked to make an introduction between colleagues. When you are on the receiving end of an introduction, remember always to close the loop.

When Away, Be Away

It can be difficult to completely pull yourself away from work obligations while at a conference. Don't miss out on this rare opportunity to be in the room with people in your field. You will need to plan ahead to be fully engaged and present.

Supervisors and co-workers need to be prepped for your time out of the office. Make sure anything you need to sign off on is done ahead of time or delegated to a qualified surrogate.

The same thing is true for clients. You'll need to be sure all major deadlines are met and they have a sense of where the projects are before you leave. Tie up as many loose ends as possible before you go to the event and put in place surrogates who can handle issues if they arise in your absence.

While at the conference, keep an eye on your inbox and voicemail but only respond to truly urgent matters. If you respond to something, which could've waited until you were back in the office, then the boundary is broken and the expectation now is you are readily available for all routine inquiries.

Your away message on your email and voicemail should say you are out of the office (if the event is well known in your industry, it may be beneficial to mention). It should also say when you will be back and who to contact in your absence. Set up a time each day you will check in with your office to answer any questions, but have someone else respond to emails and calls.

Now, confident you have a plan to handle whatever might come up back at the office, you can focus on the opportunities at this event.

GRACEFUL EXIT STRATEGIES

You've done it! You're in a conversation at the conference. You feel like it's going well and you've enjoyed chatting. The whole time you've been a little nervous because you never know how to wrap up conversations and often feel like you get stuck in them.

Going to networking events can have its challenges: For some attendees getting into a conversation is difficult, but for many wrapping up a conversation is the real challenge.

How do you know when to move on, and how do you wrap up a conversation gracefully?

MINDFULNESS

Are you feeling distracted and unable to focus on what your conversation partner is saying? Are you having difficulty maintaining eye contact with the person speaking and keep looking over their shoulder at the person who looks like, no definitely is, your ex (or boss, person you want to date or work for, best friend from third grade, etc.)? Notice this is happening. Become aware of yourself in the room. Self-awareness will help you know when it's time to wrap up the conversation.

BORED OR BORING?

Self-awareness will help you realize you are tired (or hungry, worried about the meter running out on your parking space, etc.). None of these distractions have anything to do with whether the person you're speaking with is boring.

These are about you and what's going on in your body and mind. If you need to use the restroom and the person you're speaking with is telling an exciting story, you won't register the same enthusiasm you usually would. You would appear distracted.

If you kept checking your phone to see if the babysitter has texted her check-in, you would appear bored—although this has nothing to do with how engaging your conversation partner is. Time to wrap the conversation up so you can deal with whatever is distracting you.

If you notice these signs in the person you're speaking with, it doesn't necessarily mean you're boring, but it does mean you should wrap things up.

INTERNAL CLOCK

What if you really hit it off with someone and you're having an amazing conversation? Wonderful! That's excellent. Even so, have a sense of how much time is passing. Your goal (and likely theirs) was to meet or reconnect with several people at the event, so squirreling away with one person for most of the night isn't advantageous for either of you.

Tell them you've really enjoyed the conversation and would love to stay in touch. Invite them to attend an upcoming event you have on your calendar or ask where else you might run into each other. You could even share with them that you're trying to get better at networking so you've set goals for yourself to meet more people.

END ON A HIGH NOTE

The key is to always leave them wanting more. Whether you're having a really great conversation or after a few questions realized it wasn't going anywhere, you want to leave them feeling good about you. Then when you see them later in the evening, they will naturally be inclined to introduce you to the people they are standing with.

Ask to be Introduced

If you're new to a space, a great way to wrap up a conversation is to ask to be introduced: "Do you know anyone here you think I should meet?" This usually leads to some brainstorming. When they mention a specific name, say, "Great. Will you introduce me?"

This works best if you're speaking to someone who's a regular at these events, but it could work if they even know only one other person in the room. This allows them to be a connector. They've learned a little bit about you and can use this information to try and make a great introduction to someone else at the event.

Results will vary, but this method will help you get closer to making the best connections possible in the room. It will also assist you if someone has glommed on to you at the conference, because you can always offer to make an introduction if other attempts to wrap up fail you.

I used this technique when I was at a very large convention's "after party"—where the music was too loud and the lights too low to actually network. The person I was speaking with was a college student, and I had been out of school for nearly two decades. When it became apparent we had nothing else to talk about I asked if he knew anyone else there he thinks I should meet. He lit up and asked if I wanted to meet so-and-so. I said yes, and a moment later was being pulled through the crowd up to... his intern supervisor.

He didn't have to know dozens of people I'd want to meet, just one. His supervisor was a senior executive at a nonprofit in my area and a quality contact in a vast sea of people I didn't know. The college student introduced us, I thanked him, and he walked away quite proud he had made our connection happen.

Something to keep in mind—interns work for people important enough to have interns. So don't discount the quality of the introduction based on the experience level of the person doing the introducing.

NUMBERS GAME

One other thing to keep in mind when you're trying to decide if it's time to move on is the number of people in the conversation with you. If there are three or more people in your group, you can slide away with a gesture and a murmur when others are talking. You don't need to look each person in the eye, shake their hand, and tell them you're walking away. You just say, "I'm going to go mmmm..." trailing off as you walk away. Easy as pie.

Take notice when there are only three of you because if someone other than you walks away, there will only be two of you. At this point, you need to decide whether it's time to wrap up the conversation by asking to be introduced (or offering to introduce them). You may also want to invite someone else to join you, which would then allow you to step away once they became engaged in conversation. As I said, it's far easier to gracefully step away when there are three or more people in your group.

Grip, Grin, and Go

What if it's just the two of you and you're ready to wrap up the conversation? What do you do and say to exit gracefully?

It's a three-step process that needs to be done without interruption. Start by shaking their hand (grip), then with a smile (grin), say something nice (e.g., "It was great to see you here," "I enjoyed meeting you," or "Pleasure speaking with you."), and then walk away (go).

If you've had trouble ending a conversation, it's possible you interrupted this three-step process. Have you ever shaken someone's hand, said "it was great to meet you," and then thought of something else you wanted to say?

If you say what you were thinking and then chat for a few more minutes, you've wasted the social cue of handshaking. It's entirely possible when you once again shake hands, the person you are speaking with will interrupt with a comment or question.

Yes, you're now stuck a bit, but who started it? You have some control over how successful the social cue of a handshake is. Your hands and feet need to be in sync. If you shake hands, your feet need to walk away. You can always circle back to chat with this person again later in the evening or send a follow-up email.

The goal is to leave them on a high note so they are looking forward to seeing or hearing from you again. Staying in touch is the basis of relationship building, which after all is the point of networking.

How to Follow Up

Exchanging business cards does not indicate you are establishing a relationship. Evidence of this is when you actually make plans to reconnect. So stop obsessing over collecting as many business cards as possible, because all you end up with then is a stack of business cards on your desk. Focus instead on having conversations where you leave the person wanting to talk further.

Remember, networking is about building relationships, not collecting business cards.

Are You Good at Follow Up?

Of course, actually following up is key to building relationships. When I present my Art of the Schmooze session, I ask participants to raise their hand if they are good at follow up—only a few tentative hands go up. This is why it's important to have strategic goals and a networking plan. Know before you even leave for the event why you're going and who you hope to meet.

BE PREPARED

In the "Be Strategic" section, I recommended writing a draft of your follow-up email before you go to an event. Writing this draft message will guide you through the steps of identifying who you're most excited to meet (either a specific person or a general description), what you hope to talk about, and what you want them to know about you.

You'll find a specific guide for writing this draft email in the "Resources" section.

BE CONFIDENT

Writing this email draft will also help you get in the right mindset before going to the event. You'll enter more confident and with a stronger sense of purpose. Having clear goals and a strategy will help you meet people you'll want to stay connected with after the event. Don't lose track of these priority connections.

TRACK PRIORITY CONNECTIONS

At the event, separate the cards you were handed after only a brief conversation, from the ones where you spoke in-depth. This could be different pockets or just by turning down the corner of the cards you want to prioritize.

Doing this will make it easy to identify which people you want to prioritize following up with after the event. Ideally, you would also write a note on the back of each business card to remind yourself where you met, what you discussed, and any specific follow up you had planned to do (or asked them to do).

TAKE A PHOTO

Personally, I like the physical reminder of receiving a business card, but I've also met people who have found it useful to take a picture of the business cards they want to prioritize. If you are disciplined about organizing your photos after each event, this may work well for you.

The Evernote app has several features that make it possible to scan business cards, add notes, and set reminders to follow up. With LinkedIn and Evernote integration there are even more possibilities.[11]

Even if you take home a stack of business cards from a conference, it might still be a good idea to take photos of priority business cards—so you don't risk losing them in the chaos of packing, traveling, and unpacking.

FOLLOW THROUGH

Since you already have a draft message, or perhaps have drafted several over time, and you have been keeping track of priority connections, you have set yourself up to follow through with follow up successfully.

Schedule an hour within two days of every event or conference to do your follow up. Actually put it in your calendar. Schedule this before you leave for the event so it's already on your calendar when you return to over-flowing inboxes and a long to-do list.

If possible, send messages to your priority connections while still at the event. This may lead to the opportunity to meet up again in person.

When the time comes, pull out the cards you had prioritized, open up your library of follow-up messages, and take a few minutes to personalize each message. Include a mention of where you met and what you had discussed. If you just say, "It was good to meet you at the event," this isn't very descriptive and won't help a busy networker place you.

They may not respond right away, so give them enough clues to remember you after a short delay.

Concise and Clear

Keep this message relatively brief, three short paragraphs or less. Sending longer messages often results in the recipient skimming, deciding this is an item they need to add to their to-do list, and then putting off responding. Be clear what you're asking for if you have a request.

Timing

Your outreach should be done within a short amount of time, preferably within forty-eight hours or at most two business days. We are all busy people, and likely the people you hope to connect with are even busier people. It's safe to say your brief conversation will be less memorable if you wait two weeks to send them a follow-up message.

Get Connected

My default is to send LinkedIn connection requests instead of email follow-up for all except the business cards I've prioritized. This is because I know how awkward it can be to receive a "nice to meet you" email that has no next step—do you reply, "you too"?

Instead, those random cards I received at the conference receive a LinkedIn connection request with a quick note. This leaves me time to do thoughtful follow up for the conversations which felt more meaningful and have a clear next step (e.g., to schedule a call/Skype, a podcast interview, dinner invitation).

Some people are choosy about who they connect with on LinkedIn, so it's important to send a personal note with each LinkedIn connection request. The only reliable way to see the note option is to always submit the request from their profile page—while on a computer. Reminding them where you met and what you spoke about will improve your odds of connecting.

Of course, if you already sent an email with a specific request, you can also send a LinkedIn request.

Before sending the request to connect, skim their profile to see what or who else you have in common. This will also be a good moment to see if they've been posting blog posts on their LinkedIn profile. Commenting on or sharing their blog posts would help you stay top of mind.

The other social media channel I recommend connecting with new contacts on is Twitter. This is particularly useful if they tweet regularly. Stay on their radar by "liking" and/or retweeting their tweets—or replying to them.

Sending a Facebook friend request after a brief meeting at a professional conference should not be the norm. If you connect through a professional Facebook group, then you may wish to send a request. Some people keep their Facebook list small—just family and close friends—so your friend request may not be accepted.

THAT DEVICE IN YOUR POCKET IS ALSO A PHONE

Follow up doesn't need to be high-tech to be effective. Calling people to catch up would make you stand out in a world where "liking" someone's post is considered engagement. Susan RoAne, networking expert and author of *How to Work a Room*®, calls these "make HAY while the sun shines phone calls."[12] HAY stands for, "How are ya?"

I've been trying to fit a couple of these in each week, and people have really enjoyed hearing from me out of the blue. It really is remarkable how personal a phone call is when we usually keep up with each other by reading Facebook updates or tweets.

As Susan said, "If we are a commodity or a service, we are missing the connection. The only thing that builds connections is conversation—whether online or face-to-face."[13]

Incorporate HAY calls into your life. Make a short list of six to ten people you want to reach out to, and whenever you have fifteen minutes to spare, give one of them a call. It's true, the device in your pocket actually makes phone calls and isn't just for browsing Facebook, checking email, and playing the latest game craze.

HANDWRITTEN NOTES

Another low-tech method is to send handwritten notes whenever you want to make a strong impression. This was the advice Neen James, professional speaker and a thought leader in the area of productivity, shared when I interviewed her. She said, "I think it's important as leaders to schedule connection time. So if I go to an event I schedule follow up time in my calendar so I can send thank you notes. I write a handwritten note to people when I get a business card; I send a handwritten note wherever possible."[14]

> **"I think that analog systems
> get attention in a digital world."
> —Neen James**

Travel to conferences with stationery and stamps, so you can get a jump-start on writing thank you notes while at the event or on the plane ride home. You don't need to write an essay, just a few sentences letting them know you enjoyed meeting them, remind them what you spoke about, and mention you'll be in touch via email as well.

She said, "We get about 200 emails a day, but when you get a thank you note that's what stands out. We have to be clever about how we get the attention of our network because they are all crazy busy people."[15]

Regularly Host Dinners

One of my first suggestions in this book was to host a private dinner at the conference. Hosting dinners is a great way to stay connected with people in between events as well.

Hosting private dinner parties is a strategy that has helped Dorie Clark, best-selling author of *Reinventing You* and *Stand Out*, build her professional network. By being the convener, she is providing something of value for her guests, a welcoming space where they can meet like-minded people.

Dorie very successfully did this when she moved to New York City. In a new city, surrounded by millions of busy, successful people, she began to host dinner parties for up to ten guests.

She said, "I love to organize dinners. It's a two-fold benefit—part of it is, I think it's fun for people to go to dinner where they are meeting lots of people, it's high value for them because they're investing a couple of hours, but getting to meet eight or ten really cool people."[16]

This networking technique is beneficial for Dorie, not just for her guests: "It also serves as a networking benefit for me, because I have a limited amount of time and often times there is a default in our culture to suggest 'Let's have coffee!' That's the standard thing people will suggest if they don't have a compelling reason to do otherwise. And that's nice, but if I had coffee one-on-one with all the people who wanted to, I would never have any time in my schedule."[17]

She would also be highly caffeinated.

She said, "Organizing dinner gatherings is a much better way to do it. I'm able essentially to do networking in bulk. Spending a few hours one evening every couple of weeks and getting to see tons of people, plus bringing together people from different facets of my life."[18]

ONE-ON-ONE REINED IN

As Dorie rightly pointed out, meeting for coffee with everyone who asks would leave her little time to work on her business. Of course, there are times when a one-on-one in-person conversation is incredibly helpful, and there are ways to incorporate them into your schedule without getting overwhelmed.

The person I've most admired for this is Stephanie Chung, the speaker and coach I introduced earlier. She sets aside a specific day to schedule up to seven in-person meetings. She actually spends the entire day in one location, an upscale hotel restaurant.

Starting at 8:00 a.m. she meets with clients every two hours. Her last appointment starts at 8:00 p.m. Yes, that's seven meetings in fourteen hours.

You might not have Stephanie's stamina to host seven meetings in one day, but this drive and determination are what led her to win sales awards while closing multi-million dollar deals. Apply some of her tips to your life to move toward your own audacious goals.

TRAVEL OPPORTUNITIES
Sometimes staying in one location and having people come to you isn't possible. If your job requires you to travel a lot, you might be in a different city every week.

This is true for Chris Clarke-Epstein, a change expert, author, and professional speaker. She's on the road speaking throughout the year. Despite this, she meets in person with colleagues in between conferences. She does this by keeping track of where each of these colleagues lives and coordinates meeting up with them whenever she is going to be within driving distance from their home.[19]

SOCIAL MEDIA HAS ITS LIMITS

Scott Stratten, best-selling author of "UnMarketing: Stop Marketing, Start Engaging" and host of the UnPodcast, was named one of the Top 5 Social Media Influencers in the world by Forbes.com, said it best: "Nothing beats face-to-face. Virtual is not a substitute for face-to-face, it's an addition or an enhancement."[20]

While social media does allow us to keep tabs on each other, it is not as helpful at deepening relationships. As Scott said, "Never substitute virtual for in-person. Nothing beats it. Virtual helps keep the connection going in between the in-person ones. It's really important, and I would tell this to anyone who thinks they can just do this from their phone."[21]

DON'T WASTE YOUR TIME

These are just some ways you can stay connected after you meet someone. Try something new or stick with what feels most comfortable. Just do something. If you regularly go to events, collect lots of business cards, and don't send any follow-up messages, you are definitely wasting your time networking.

Try to stay in touch even when you don't need something, this could be a quick note of encouragement before a big event a contact is hosting or congratulations after they publish a book.

Set a Google alert for your key contacts so you'll know when they are in the news, or keep an eye on the updates from LinkedIn. But don't let too much time pass for your most important relationships and the ones you hope will become significant.

USING TECHNOLOGY

I remember attending my first conference over twenty years ago. The event had over two-dozen concurrent breakouts to choose from during each 90-minute session. I stayed up very, very late the first night trying to figure out my schedule for the next few days. I had this complicated symbol system to help me track how interested I was in each breakout and then prioritized my top three for each session. It took hours and hours, and I was not well rested for the very full days ahead.

I still attend this conference, but now I spend time looking through all the breakout descriptions in advance and save them using the event app. I can even save the ones I'm prioritizing right into my Google Calendar, so at the last minute, I know what my plan B is if my first choice session is full or isn't the right fit.

EVENT APP
Be sure you're taking full advantage of all the features of your event app. For starters, sign in so you can create

your own schedule. Can't decide between two sessions? While you can't be in two places at once, you can download the handouts for the sessions you miss. Do a little research about the speakers before you attend, and perhaps this will help you prioritize.

And don't forget to fill out your profile on the attendee section so your fellow attendees can learn more about you and connect. Link your social accounts if the option is available, so attendees can easily find you on LinkedIn and Twitter.8

> **Don't just show up and wing it.**
> **Make this your conference.**

GMAIL INBOX TOOLS

One of my best networking tips is to draft your follow-up email BEFORE going to the event. I explain how to do this in detail in the "Resources" section. If you use Gmail, you can use Canned Responses to keep track of these draft email messages. Over time you will create a library of messages you can tweak before each event.

Canned Responses is a Gmail feature that enables you to easily insert a sentence, paragraph, or even several paragraphs into a new email. It will save you a lot of time when sending follow-up messages, answers to frequently asked questions, or any other evergreen content. Canned Responses are also useful if you have different email signatures depending on who you are corresponding with or don't want to have your full email signature in every reply email.

This feature is available through Gmail Labs, that are experimental features Google offers in beta. To enable any Gmail Lab feature, click the gear icon in the top right of the Gmail pane. Go to Settings, then Labs and scroll down to Canned Responses, select the Enable radio button, and click Save Changes.

Once you've enabled this feature, creating a canned response is simple. From your inbox, click Compose, and type a reply you want to save. Next, click the arrow in the lower right corner of the message window and select Canned Responses > New Canned Response. Name the response, and click OK.

When you want to use a canned response, click the arrow again from the message you're replying to, and select Canned Response, then the name of the one you want to insert.

Undo Send

You probably noticed other useful Gmail Labs while scrolling. They change frequently, so check back to see if any new ones pop up that you might want to use. Unfortunately, this also means some Labs you love may disappear. The good news is Labs sometimes become permanent features of Gmail.

Undo Send, one of my favorites Gmail Labs, became a permanent feature. Undo Send gives you time to cancel an email after you've hit send. Very handy when right after you hit send, you realize you spelled someone's name wrong. You'll find this and other useful features in Settings.

TWITTER

Standing out doesn't always require standing in the front of the room or taking on a volunteer role. Stand out by actively tweeting throughout the conference. Even if you're not active on Twitter the rest of the year, you can use this tool to connect with fellow attendees and become known by the organizers.

Twitter is especially useful at large events. It's a back channel where you can listen in on sessions you're not attending, because someone in the session is live tweeting great takeaways. You can also learn about informal socials or pop-up sessions. The people who actively tweet will become familiar to you, and you'll feel like you know them if you meet in person.

Tina Capalbo, a social media and brand storytelling expert, shared her Twitter conference networking strategy: "Get into the habit of asking people you meet if they're on Twitter. When you exchange business cards, ask for their @TwitterName, and write it on their card. Then tweet hello later that day. Sometimes there's an opportunity to open the Twitter app and look them up during your conversation. Some people are very agile with their phones. Timing is everything. Connecting for the first time online while, or just after, meeting someone face-to-face is always more meaningful."[22]

NOT FAMILIAR WITH HOW TO USE TWITTER?

For starters, if you haven't yet, visit www.Twitter.com and sign up for an account. You'll need to choose a username (e.g., @RobbieSamuels). Then take a few minutes to add a profile picture and brief bio. Don't skip adding a photo and bio; doing so is like giving someone a blank business card—not very useful. Then, download an app to your phone so you can easily follow the event hashtag (e.g., #hashtag) and tweet while on the go.

TWITTER PRO TIP

If you tweet from multiple accounts, download separate apps for each account rather than switch accounts while in one app. This helps avoid accidentally tweeting from the wrong account. I tweet from three different Twitter accounts, so I use the Twitter app, Hootsuite app, and UberSocial app to be sure I'm tweeting from the correct account each time.

Tweet Before You Meet

Start following the event hashtag a couple of weeks before the conference. At first there will be only a few tweets now and again, but this will increase as you get closer to opening night. If you decide to post your own tweets, make sure you always include the event hashtag. This way your tweets will be included in the search results when someone searches the event hashtag.

Power of a Retweet

If you're new to Twitter, you can focus on retweeting posts that resonate with you. The person who sent the tweet will appreciate you amplifying their message. If you're the person whose message has been retweeted, take the time to reply and say thank you.

Tweet Takeaways

One thing I like to do during the event is to post specific takeaways I learn at the conference, tips I believe others would benefit from hearing. I usually do this after I've culled through my notes for the day and I'm wrapping things up at night.

Tweeting takeaways helps me leave the event with a short list of actionable steps I plan to take in the next two weeks, rather than just a long and jumbled list of notes from all the sessions I attended. It also has had the extra benefit of leading to interesting conversations on- and off-line based on the tweets I posted.

TWEET THANKS

Tweet to thank speakers and organizers. Ideally, Twitter handles for speakers will be available on a place card in front of them when they are speaking. Do some research ahead of the event and send a tweet to a few speakers you are particularly looking forward to hearing speak. Your name will be more familiar when you say a quick hello at the beginning of the session.

TWITTER LISTS

Another suggestion from Tina Capalbo, is to "create a *public* Twitter list beforehand. Give your list a relevant and appealing name in 25 characters or less, something like: People to Meet at #ConferenceHashtag or Looking Forward to #ConferenceHashtag. When the people you add to your list get notified, the name of your list will help them understand why you connected with them and what you have in common. Curating this list will save you browsing time during the event, reduce feed-noise and distraction, and allow you to focus on timely conference conversations."[23]

Twitter lists are a great way to stay in touch after the event. Retweet messages that resonate with you to stay connected in between events. This can be especially useful in the few weeks before the next event, so you can remind yourself who you are looking forward to seeing again and get back on their radar.

SELFIES

Another fun way to use Twitter is to share selfies while at the event. If you have a particularly great conversation, ask if you can take a selfie, then tweet the image using their Twitter handle and the event hashtag. Event organizers love seeing this kind of engagement, so don't be surprised if your tweet gets retweeted by them or included in marketing for next year's event.

Another option is to share the photo via email when you send your follow-up message. If your photos are backed up to the cloud (e.g., Google Photos), you can share the link to the image instead of sending lots of large files from your inbox.

Sharing selfies will make you more memorable. You will also have an easier time connecting names and faces when you get home to send follow-up messages.

TECH TO TRACK

As of the writing of this book, LinkedIn went through a major update, that resulted in a lot of helpful features being removed from the free version. Two of those features were the ability to tag a profile and write private notes. Unfortunately, if you were using these features before the update, you lost access to this information unless you upgraded your account.

Fortunately, there is another tech solution. The Chrome plug-in Dux-Soup integrates with LinkedIn and enables you to tag profiles and write private notes. With this plug-in, LinkedIn once again becomes a simple contact relationship management (CRM) tool. There is a free option that lets you write notes for every profile you visit.

The paid version also allows you to download a spreadsheet that includes the tags and notes you wrote for your priority contacts. For instance, if you were creating a shortlist of people you hope to stay in touch with after a conference. You could tag those profiles, write a brief note, and then view them periodically. This keeps those contacts from getting lost among the rest of your connections.

If you have a free LinkedIn account and have found it difficult to track your top contacts, you should consider the professional Dux-Soup package. As an affiliate, I'm able to share a special offer – 6-month package includes one month free or 12-month package includes three months free.

Learn more at www.robbiesamuels.com/dux-soup. You'll also find this information in the 'Resources' section for easy reference.

TECH TO RECONNECT

Relationships are built over time, but this doesn't mean it should take a lot of time to coordinate meeting up again. I use a ScheduleOnce booking form to reduce the number of back-and-forth emails necessary to schedule an in-person meeting, video chat, or phone call. There are several other services available that integrate with Google calendar.

Using a booking form, I can set specific hours I'm willing to schedule meetings, and if those times are free on my calendar, they are offered when someone wants to schedule time with me.

Because I have a booking form, I feel much more open to inviting people to connect with me. For instance, I have a form to schedule a twenty-minute chat, which is ideal for quick check-ins or if someone has a question. This is what I offer if someone asks me to meet for coffee, saving me a lot of travel and meeting time when I don't know someone very well.

If I know I want to have more time to meet either in person or virtually, I send a different link to schedule a thirty-minute to two-hour meeting. The form requests their cell phone number, so I'm no longer scrambling to find their number if plans need to change last minute or I've arrived at the meeting place but don't spot them.

As a podcast host, I have found booking forms make it easy for my guests to schedule (and reschedule) their interviews, and I'm able to request additional information, like their bio, headshot, and social media links.

As you can see, there are many ways booking forms can minimize the time it takes to schedule meetings. Set one up so you can freely invite the people you meet at conferences to connect with you afterward.

STAY TOP OF MIND

You dutifully sent your follow-up emails, sent LinkedIn requests, and followed them on Twitter. What next?

You need a system for staying in touch periodically. A simple method is to use labels in Gmail to tag your follow-up emails. You can add several tags to identify what conference you met at, what city they live in, and also a tag to track when you're waiting for a reply.

Tagging what city they live in is a tip I picked up from Ramit Sethi[24], best-selling author, entrepreneur, and personal finance advisor. When he travels for work, he can quickly and easily search his inbox to find people who live in his destination city.

If you also tag new contacts with a specific conference, you'll remember where you met even after several months have passed. Meeting up again in person is a great way to build on your previous connections.

KEEPING IN TOUCH

There is a difference between meeting people and keeping in touch, which is often harder in practice than you'd think. To help me manage my most meaningful relationships, and ones I hope will become significant, I use Contactually, a robust CRM perfect for managing my network.

I put each contact into a "bucket" that correlates to how frequently I want to be in touch. When this amount of time has passed, if I have not reconnected, the contact's name appears on my dashboard.

What I appreciate most about Contactually is it helps me stay in touch with my weakest links: the contacts where I don't have a specific project to work together on, but I value what they do and don't want them to slip away.

Sign up for a free trial by using my affiliate link: www.robbiesamuels.com/contactually. Let me know if you do, and I'll help you get set up for success. You'll also find this information in the 'Resources' section for easy reference.

BE INCLUSIVE

WHY CROISSANTS VS. BAGELS?

BAGELS

Quite a bit of the conference takes place outside of breakout sessions, so you'll need to know how to navigate the vibrant chaos of the hallway and crowded receptions. I've been leading sessions on networking for nearly a decade, and what I'm about to share is by far my most memorable takeaway, and thus the title of this book. It's about body language and what you can do to help make the conference a more welcoming and inclusive space.

Picture this: on the first day of the conference, there is a thirty-minute block on the schedule for networking. You gamely head into the hallway, grab a cup of coffee, and begin to circle the space looking for an opening for your first conversation. You are not having a lot of success because everyone around you is in tight networking circles. These shoulder-to-shoulder huddles are the "bagels"—they are round and it is nearly impossible to break into them.

If you are like most people, you'll be looking for an easy opening. Not seeing one, you might circle the room and then head to your next breakout session early. If you do this, you will be missing out on all of the possible connections happening in the hallway between sessions.

WALLFLOWERS

If it feels too early to go to the next breakout session, you might be drawn to the person standing alone against the wall. If this is your first time at this conference, I wouldn't suggest talking to wallflowers. Even if it is a great conversation, the ending is going to be very awkward. Neither of you knows other people at the event, so you can't make introductions. Your best bet is to engage with attendees chatting in small groups .

CROISSANTS

Now imagine you're one of the people standing in a typical networking "bagel." If you took a small step back with one foot and turned your torso slightly, you'd create an opening, which would make it easier for someone to join your group. That is the "croissant"—the opening to help someone join the conversation.

WHY WOULD YOU WANT TO BE EASY TO APPROACH?

You are at this conference to meet people, right? Or else you could have stayed home and just purchased an online course to learn the same material.

How Do You Stand So
You're Easy to Approach?

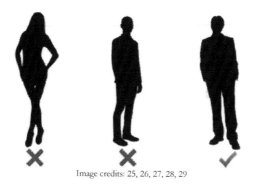

Image credits: 25, 26, 27, 28, 29

Some people stand with their feet crossed. To move in any direction, they would first need to untangle their feet, step in one direction, and then start moving. This stance doesn't make you approachable, and you may find it's harder to move in and out of group conversations.

Others stand with their feet shoulder width apart. If you are talking to only one other person and want others to join your conversation, this stance isn't very welcoming.

CLOSED OR OPEN BODY LANGUAGE?

There are times when you don't want anyone to interrupt your conversation. Perhaps you finally got some face time with a key influencer in your field and you know others are circling to jump in at the first opportunity to do so. In those moments, your body language should be closed. However, those moments of having closed body language should not be your default.

Align your body language
with your intentions.

We've established you are at the conference to meet people. So make sure you are easy to approach. Stand with your feet shoulder-width apart, one leg back a bit, with your weight on the back leg, torso turned slightly toward whichever foot is in the back.

Now you are approachable and can easily invite anyone passing by to join in the conversation.

"EVERYONE WAS SO FRIENDLY!"

This simple physical act is one of the best ways to navigate an event and create a welcoming community space. I've found only a small percentage of attendees need to be practicing this and the effect will begin to be felt by everyone. They'll leave wondering why this event felt so friendly and welcoming.

BAGELS WITH LOX

But let's say you're approaching a "bagel" and no one in the circle seems to have a clue you are there and trying to join the conversation. What do you do? Try to get the attention of just one of the people in the group and step into the circle next to them.

If you're an outgoing extrovert, you might be inclined to take over a conversation—don't.

> **Just because you can,
> doesn't mean you should.**

SCAN FOR CROISSANTS

You don't have to start by breaking into these tight networking huddles. When you first get to the networking space, look around the room, check how everyone is standing, and see if you can spot someone with a more open stance. Just focus on one of the people in the circle, and as the group conversation continues, begin a side conversation with the person who made space for you. And of course, use your own body language to welcome others into your new conversation.

BE WELCOMING

If you are in one of those tight networking circles and you see someone hovering nearby, turn to create space for them to join you. If someone approaches your "croissant" and seems hesitant, wave them in. When there is a pause in the conversation, let the newcomer know what you are discussing. "Bob was just telling us about his trip to Alaska." This gracious gesture allows the newcomer to listen politely and then ask relevant questions.

What Exactly Is the Stance?

Image credits: 30, 31, 32

Start with your feet shoulder-width apart, then move one foot half a step back and put your weight on your back leg. Turn your back leg slightly—either toward two o'clock or ten o'clock. It is not an overly exaggerated or wide stance, just a subtle shift in your body language. This will have a profound impact on how easily people approach you and your ability to navigate the room.

Share this tip so you and your colleagues can remind each other to "stop bageling." It's a sticky concept— kind of like croissants and jam.

ROLE OF HOSTS

The fastest way to becoming known in a new space is to attend events regularly. Sporadic attendance will leave you feeling like you need to keep starting from scratch when meeting people at these events. For conferences, this means committing to attending several years in a row before deciding "whether it's worth it."

BENEFITS OF BEING A REGULAR

Showing up consistently and participating actively will help you become better known by other regular attendees and familiar to the organizers. Once you've established rapport with the organizers and other regular attendees, they will be more willing and able to help introduce you to the people in the room you have not yet met. They will know more about you and your goals, which may lead them to make important introductions on your behalf without any prompting.

You can see how having a team of people aware of your goals and helping you make connections would make these events feel much more effective than the ones where you barely know a soul. All it takes is showing up consistently, demonstrating the type of interaction you want by being warm and friendly, and having a clear sense of purpose.

BE A HOST

Having committed to becoming a regular attendee, there are other steps you can take to become well known and appreciated in a room. You step into the role of a host. I don't mean you need to start hosting your own events, although that is a very good idea. I mean stepping up into a host role at any event where you are a regular attendee.

Hosts help other people in the room connect with each other.

This means you actively make introductions between people who might have something in common and even between two strangers sitting near each other in a breakout session. (They might end up finding something in common after all.)

When you are in one of those tight networking circles, you are aware of the people trying to find their way in— and you make space for them or wave them in. Then you make them feel welcome by letting them know what your group has been discussing.

Hosts keep an eye out for newcomers who are clinging to the sides of the room.

Earlier I said approaching wallflowers might not be the best strategy for first-time attendees. For regulars, this is an excellent plan. You won't feel stuck at the end of the conversation because you know lots of other people in the room and can always wrap up the conversation by making an introduction.

You can also wave over anyone standing nearby and include them in your chat, then step away once the two people are engaged in conversation. As a long-time attendee, you have a lot more comfort in the room than the first-time attendee standing by the wall. As a host, you can help first-time attendees feel more connected and engaged.

NOT ALL WALLFLOWERS

While we're on the topic of wallflowers, I want to remind you that just because someone is a first-time attendee and standing by the edge of the room, it doesn't mean they are new to your field. They may be very experienced, but they haven't been to this particular conference and are feeling a bit unsure of how to break into the vibrant conversations happening all around them.

I ventured over to someone standing by themselves at a conference, and the first-time attendee I met was the CEO of the newest corporate sponsor for the event. We chatted for a few minutes, he joined me for lunch, and later in the day I was able to introduce him to a board member for the association. The sponsor felt welcomed and was enthusiastic about returning the following year. I wasn't officially connected to the association, just a regular attendee who noticed the CEO standing by himself.

> Hosts are great listeners who focus their energy on the other person and become sought-after company.

Host a Table

One opportunity to host is during lunch; instead of sitting with someone you know very well, sit at an empty table. Then make eye contact with people as they are wandering around clearly looking for a place to sit. Wave them over with a smile. Continue to do this until you've filled most of your table.

By then, the people who came over will be deep in conversation, and you'll be credited for any connections that take place over lunch. When these attendees see you later in the hallway, they will go out of their way to welcome you into their tight networking circle.

If being a host sounds great to you then you will want to read the next section, where I share what questions to avoid when meeting someone.

The Downside to Being a Unicorn

Effectively and inclusively networking isn't just about body language. It's also about what we say, especially right after we meet someone.

The thing is, sometimes the very questions we ask have the opposite effect of welcoming. They are off-putting and result in feeling "othered."

Have you heard this quote?

> **"Always be yourself, unless you can be a unicorn, then always be a unicorn."**

Let's say for a moment you could be a unicorn. What would your day be like? Are you picturing rainbows and sunny skies? More likely you'd spend your day hearing, "Wow! A unicorn. I've never met a unicorn. What's it like to...?" followed by lots of curious questions.

Many of us have had this experience. We've walked into a room of strangers feeling awkward and out of place. We've felt like we're the only odd one out in the room, different from everyone else in some important way.

We are momentarily grateful when a stranger approaches us and begins a conversation. We've been saved from standing by ourselves! We begin to second-guess how fortunate we are when out of the gate, one of their first comments is:

- "Wow! You're so tall. How tall are you?"

- "Your hair is so...Can I touch it?" (their hand is already entangled in your hair)

- "You've got such great skin. Beautiful mocha color. So lucky."

- "I've never heard of anyone with your name. So exotic."

These all seem like compliments, but in practice, they are calling out people's differences. The result is you are more likely to feel "othered" than welcomed. Especially if the feature they just commented on is the same feature that always gets commented on by strangers.

CAN I TOUCH?

If you were a unicorn, you'd have people touching your horn all the time without more than a cursory request for permission. It doesn't even have to be a rare feature for someone to want to move into your personal space. This touching without permission happens to pregnant people quite often, and pregnancy is far from rare—or we wouldn't all be here.

WHERE ARE YOU FROM?

If you were a unicorn, people would ask, "Where are you from?" And when you answered, "New Jersey," they'd say, "No, I mean, where are your parents from?" You'd answer, "Oh, they're from California and Texas."

But what they're *really* asking is where did your family emigrate from. This is not something you'd think to ask a person who wasn't a unicorn and didn't in some way stand out because of their difference.

But, But... It Was Meant as a Compliment

Maybe the way you've experienced this hasn't been quite so overt. Perhaps you tend to share a lot of features with other people in the room, so your differences don't stand out quite so much. It may then be jarring to learn these conversation starters aren't received as compliments.

A compliment is when you say something nice about a feature that someone else chose. For example, the answer to any of the following observations can simply be a sincere "thank you," and the conversation is off to an upbeat start:

- "I love the color of your jacket!"

- "Your necklace is beautiful. Did you get it while traveling?"

- "You've got great style. Where do you shop?"

- "Those frames look really great on you."

Did They Choose It?

These are different than the first examples because the comment is about something chosen, rather than a curious comment or question based on who we are. We don't choose our height, skin color, accent, or myriad other features that make all of us unique.

Avoid Curious Questions

Before uttering the first thought that comes into your head when meeting someone, check first to be sure you're not asking merely out of curiosity. You've noticed something different about the person in front of you and you're about to hone in on this difference by asking about it.

Since this likely happens to this person all day, every day, they'll give you a pat answer which likely won't lead to further discussion. You won't make a great or long-lasting impression, and you'll miss the opportunity to engage with them in a meaningful way.

Put yourself in their shoes for a moment. Remember you've felt like the only odd one out in the room.

What Do You Say Instead?

My preferred opening line is, "Hi, my name is Robbie." I usually follow up by asking someone how they heard about the event. This gives them an opportunity to share a little bit about themselves. You could ask about the session you both just attended or what they are most looking forward to this weekend—any open-ended question you would feel comfortable answering yourself.

Those top-of-mind curious questions will need to wait until you've become friends and are ready to share about your differences too. Then it will feel like you're deepening your relationship and not just being curious in a "Wow! You're a unicorn. I've never met a unicorn," kind of way.

Avoid Assumptions

We've been told to avoid assumptions our entire life, yet it's human nature to default to making assumptions and generalizations. One particular assumption we tend to make is everyone we meet is straight and if they have a partner their partner is of the opposite gender. Clearly, this is not the case 100 percent of the time, so it's best to avoid language that makes this assumption. Use "partner" or "significant other" and you will avoid assumptions needing an awkward correction.

Another assumption we make is we can easily and quickly determine a person's gender. While this is likely true most of the time, you can avoid mispronouning someone by saying "they" when speaking about someone whose gender presentation makes their gender identity less obvious. The use of "they" as a singular, gender-neutral pronoun has become more popular and is even used by the Associated Press.[33]

TREAT FIRST-TIMERS AS VIPS

Many associations have seen a decline over the last two decades in membership and attendance at their annual conventions. It's no longer required to attend an in-person event to learn new skills or even to "meet" influencers.

Add to this the differences in how each generation prefers to network and learn. These factors have made it even more important that those who do attend in-person events find them incredibly valuable, so they will plan to return the following year.

OVERWHELMED

Ask first-time attendees to sum up their experience thus far at a large conference or convention, and it's likely they will say "overwhelmed." The vibrant culture of the event combined with the sheer number of sessions to choose from leads to this feeling of overwhelm.

How quickly first-time attendees feel fully integrated and welcomed into the space factors heavily in whether they move past this initial feeling and begin to embrace the vibrant culture of the event. When this happens, they begin to find connections and build relationships with other attendees.

RETENTION

Retaining first-time attendees is a high priority for conference organizers. It should also be a high priority for long-time attendees since the ongoing success and sustainability of the event (and possibly the association) depends on a fair number of first-time attendees returning year after year.

Treat first-timers as VIPs; a title usually bestowed only on those who are receiving an award, have paid special fees, or achieved a particularly high status in their field. Bearing in mind how expensive it can be to recruit new members and the importance of retaining membership, you can begin to see why treating first-time attendees as VIPs is an important principle.

VIP RIBBONS

I saw this principle in action at Influence, the National Speakers Association's annual conference. First-time attendees were given VIP ribbons to wear on their name badges.

Nate Riggs, professional speaker and CEO of NR Media Group, wrote a blog post about his experience as a VIP at Influence. He said, "The unique VIP approach ensures that new members are welcomed by groups of people who understand and hold sacred the culture of the association."[34]

If you have been attending a conference for several years, you may not have realized that you and other long-time attendees are the keepers of the event's culture. The degree of welcoming spirit experienced by first-time attendees will color their perception of the event, the association, and if they are new to the field, perhaps even their chosen career path.

IT'S NOT ABOUT THE RIBBONS

VIP ribbons, or any other symbol, make it easy for first-time attendees to be identified. Helpful, yes; however, the real test is how long-time attendees treat them.

If you are a long-time attendee and notice a first-timer nearby, ask them how the event is going for them. "What has been the highlight of the conference for you so far?" Ask if they'd like some advice on how to navigate this awesome event, and if they are interested, then share your best tips.

Remember what it was like your first time attending this event? The feeling of being overwhelmed and not knowing quite where to go or who to meet?

Now, after attending for five or more years, the event feels like a reunion but this didn't happen the first, second, or possibly even the third year.

Warm Welcome

Welcome first-time attendees into the conference family. Don't target them with offers of coaching services, courses, or other professional services. If you have something of value to offer, wait until they are asking for information that aligns with the services or products you represent, and start by sharing free advice.

Instill in them a sense of pride about being part of this association. Pay forward the introductions and warm welcome you (hopefully) received your first couple of years at this event.

You never know—you might be greeting a future association president!

Communicating Across Difference

Creating a welcoming event is a multi-faceted endeavor, and I would be remiss if I did not offer some guidance on how to communicate with a person with a disability. Unfortunately, the angst people have about networking gets amplified when given the opportunity to connect with those with disabilities. This may be true even if you have a disability yourself.

Some people choose to avoid engaging rather than do or say something wrong. Others make an awkward, hesitant effort, that is sometimes perceived as inconsiderate and rather than making someone feel included may have the exact opposite effect.

The bottom line is to be respectful.

Aside from that basic tenet of respect, there are some things to keep in mind when communicating with someone who is differently-abled than you.

CURIOUS QUESTIONS

I've already driven this point home, but it bears repeating: just as you shouldn't comment on how tall someone is or zero in on any other feature they have no control over, don't ask the curious question that pops into your head when you first meet someone with a disability. You will get a rote response, and it won't lead to a more engaging conversation.

Kari Turner, a writer and disability activist, shared she's "noticed that folks have a tendency to think it's perfectly okay to ask personal questions. They don't seem to understand that when you ask about a person's disability, you are asking about their body. End of story. Inquiring point-blank about my ability to stand for long periods of time is not a way to greet me. Asking the name of my 'condition' is not the way to find out my name. If you want to greet me, just say hello. If you want to learn my name, try telling me yours."[35]

To Shake or Not to Shake?

I've already stressed how important handshakes are as a social cue. So you might be thrown off if you meet someone who isn't able to shake hands for one reason or another. The social cue works even if the person has an artificial limb, arm only to their elbow, or very limited hand use. Even a gesture without any physical contact still works as a social cue. In some cases it may be more appropriate to shake with your left hand. When in doubt, let the person you're talking to take the lead to show you what would be most comfortable.

Who Are You Talking To?

Interpreters and companions are not who you are trying to meet. Therefore, don't direct your question to them. Maintain eye contact with the person with a disability so they know you are waiting for them to respond.

Can I Help You?

One of the ways people who are temporarily able-bodied interact with people with disabilities is to offer assistance. The instinct to help is great. Just be sure this particular person wants your help. This means you need to wait for a response before jumping in with unsolicited support. Listen carefully to the response so you can follow specific instructions. The onus is on the person with the disability to ask for help, not for you to offer.

MS. SMITH OR MARY?

"Treat adults as adults," said Glenda Watson Hyatt, a motivational speaker who offered guidance for this section of the book. She said, "Address people who have disabilities by their first names only when extending the same familiarity to all others."[36]

This also means we should avoid other infantilizing gestures, such patting people on the head or shoulder if they are using a wheelchair, or offering to pick up someone who is much smaller than ourselves.

No. Just no.

A WHEELCHAIR IS NOT FURNITURE

It's tempting to rest against a wheelchair if you're tired of standing. To the person using the wheelchair, it feels like you are leaning directly on them. If there wasn't a wheelchair, you wouldn't think to move into someone's personal space like this. Same rules apply here then. Glenda offers one caveat, "If, however, you need to steady yourself for a moment, simply ask first."[37]

THE GOAL IS UNDERSTANDING

If the person you are speaking with has difficulty with verbal communication, ask fewer open-ended questions and focus instead on ones that can be answered "yes" or "no." You could also ask if they would like to write their response either on a piece of paper or by using a device.

Be patient as they do this. What you don't want to do is finish sentences for them, which may come across as impatience, or act as if they make perfect sense when you have no idea what they are saying. It would be best if you repeated what you heard and gave an opportunity to clarify or confirm.

NECK STRAIN IS NO JOKE

Imagine you are sitting in a chair and everyone around you is standing. The person standing to your left is engaging you in a conversation, so you're awkwardly turning to look up at them. How long could you hold this position before your neck and back ached? Okay, so now you can imagine why lowering yourself to eye level when speaking to someone in a wheelchair is so helpful. Kneel down or look around for a chair to sit in to be sure you are not towering over the person as you are speaking. This also could be perceived to be a power play, an unfortunate dynamic which will not help build a strong connection.

READ MY LIPS

Not all people who are deaf can read lips, so you'll need to ask if this would help. Get their attention by either waving your hand or lightly tapping on their shoulder. Of course, if you are standing in a dark corner it will make reading lips harder—as will speaking very quickly, eating, drinking, or smoking.

Basically, make sure you are well lit, that you keep your mouth clear of objects, and be sure you are turned toward the person who is deaf.

WHAT?

If a person is hard of hearing, they may need to situate themselves so the ear they hear best out of is closer to you. If you are aware of this, be mindful when choosing where you are sitting.

WRITTEN MIGHT BE BEST

Sometimes, the easiest way to communicate is using paper and pen or a device to share words or phrases. If someone is having a hard time understanding you, type your comment or question in a notepad on your phone.

YOU STILL THERE?

Most times, if you want to exit a conversation gracefully, it's easiest to do so when you are in a group of three or more people. You can step away with barely a murmur. Of course, if one of the people in the group is blind, then be sure they realize you are stepping away. This is especially true if you are speaking one-on-one with a person who is blind. Ducking away, even momentarily, to grab your drink off the bar or greet someone who just walked in, will leave the person who is blind standing by themselves without knowing where you went or even knowing you've left.

Oops! Did I Just Say/Do That?

"Great to see you!" or "Did you hear about…?"—are you anxious about avoiding these common expressions when speaking with a person who is blind or deaf? It's okay. Don't make it a big deal. Pointing it out and discussing your feelings is what you want to avoid. This puts a burden on the person with a disability, and for them, this is just life. It's not the first time they've heard this expression, and it won't be the last.

"I was so excited to meet Paul. I knew him by reputation but did not know the details of his disability. Fortunately, I was looking him in the eye as I reached out to shake hands, which is when I realized he didn't have the use of his hands. I simply put my hand down, kept looking him in the eye, and we proceeded to have a great conversation"—Kari Turner, recounting her first meeting with Paul Longmore, a major figure in the disability rights movement.[38]

This gaffe happened early in Kari's career, and she realizes now that Paul would have been gracious no matter her response, but by not making it a big deal she was able to make a stronger connection. One lesson she learned is you can't always predict what challenges you will uncover when networking, but we do have control over how we respond to these challenges.

Hidden Disabilities

Sometimes it's not immediately obvious that the person you are speaking with has a disability. If someone keeps asking you to repeat yourself, it's possible they are hard of hearing, and you can suggest moving the conversation to a quieter location. Try to keep an open mind and not judge someone because they have a weak handshake; it's possible it would be painful to squeeze. Have compassion if someone seems completely fine the first day of the conference and on the second day they are having a hard time standing for long periods of time; it's possible they could be experiencing flare-up from chronic pain.

It's Time to Go

Social cues are a huge part of networking, and for people with autism this is a challenge. I remember speaking with someone and at the end of the conversation I shook his hand, said it was nice to chat with him, and then I hesitated. I didn't walk away. I was waiting for him to acknowledge the social cue. To acknowledge I was leaving. After a few more minutes of chatting, I realized I was in control of the situation and didn't have to wait for him to respond. I shook his hand, said I'm going to go now, and walked away.

Later we became friendly, and he told me he had autism (then defined as Asperger's), and I asked him about this particular interaction. I asked if he had still been standing there because I was standing there. He simply said, "Yeah." I had felt so rude and abrupt walking away without him acknowledging it by saying, "Nice to see you too." He told me he appreciated how explicit I had been. He spends a lot of time not quite sure of what the socially correct response is, but with me, he knew I was going, and it was clear.

Lesson learned. If a person with autism doesn't understand social cues, then take the lead. This is also true if you are speaking to a person from another culture who may be unfamiliar with the social cue you are using. It even works if you are speaking with someone who is being obtuse and self-centered or is inebriated. The point is—you should not feel stuck in the conversation if someone isn't getting the hint you are ready to move on. It's up to you to take care of yourself and exit the conversation, even if it feels rude in the moment.

Ask

Don't avoid people with disabilities if you have the opportunity to make a connection at a conference (or elsewhere). As Glenda said, "Don't be afraid to ask questions when you're unsure what to do."[39]

If you have a disability, don't hesitate to ask for what you need to be present and engaged in the room. If you need someone to speak louder, or need to move to a quieter

space, or need to move a conversation over to chairs—
you need to be your own advocate.

CONFERENCE ETHOS

Networking is a high priority for most conference
attendees. Yet, many attendees, especially first-time
attendees, find it difficult to navigate the vibrant chaos of
the hallway between sessions.

How can event organizers shift the culture of the
conference to make it easier for attendees to engage with
each other?

"HERE WITH COLLEAGUES? GO MINGLE.
HERE ALONE? DON'T STAY THAT WAY."

If the phrase above is woven throughout the conference,
it will be much, much easier to meet new people and feel
engaged in the vibrant culture. I work with association
executives and conference planners to weave this
message into the program, including the First Timers
Orientation, remarks from the main stage, on the first
slide of every breakout session PowerPoint, and on a
signboard as attendees enter the ballroom for lunch.

I design pre-conference webinars to help attendees make
the most of the opportunities available at the conference.
This includes specific steps to create a strategic plan and

tips on how to be effective and inclusive. A separate webinar is available for everyone affiliated with the event (e.g., speakers, host committee, exhibitors, board, and staff). This webinar is focused on sharing the benefits of having a host mentality and specific steps to implement to create a welcoming event where attendees can more easily find valuable connections which make this event the "must-attend" event of the year.

While working with event planners to design these webinars, I'm also coaching them on techniques and tools to implement on an institutional level (e.g., VIP ribbons, conversation tables, networking tags). These features have a direct impact on how easily attendees, especially first-time attendees, engage with each other and feel connected to the conference culture.

To reinforce this message, I am available to present a keynote or a breakout session, host networking breaks, lead the First-Timers Orientation, and participate in the welcome remarks on opening night. Essentially, I am the ambassador for first-timers to help them navigate the vibrant culture at a conference.

Do you know someone who hosts a conference or convention? I would welcome being introduced to association executives, conference organizers, and meeting planners. Please see "About this Author" for ways to connect with me. Thank you!

COACH YOUR COLLEAGUES

Even if the phrase, "Here with colleagues? Go mingle. Here alone? Don't stay that way," isn't on the Power-Point slide as you enter a breakout session or on a signboard by the lunch buffet line, you can live this mantra by coaching your team before the event.

You and your colleagues are attending this conference for a lot of different reasons, one of which is to broaden your network. If your team sits together at lunch or huddles in the hallway, you are making the possibility of achieving this goal much more difficult.

Prior to attending the conference have a brainstorming session to create team and individual goals for this particular event. Doing this together will help each of you be accountable and potentially receive assistance during the event.

Knowing each other's goals will help remind you to break up your clique during the networking break and not to sit together during lunch. You can take advantage of the opportunity to meet peers from other organizations instead of recapping the morning with the people you see all the time at work.

CONCLUSION

What if you take to heart all of the networking tips I've shared in this book? Let's paint the picture of strategic, effective, and inclusive relationship building.

To get started, you take the time to get clear about your goals for networking and identify a few specific outcomes you are working toward. A colleague recommends a conference because they know your goals and have attended the event a few times. You spend some time looking over the organization's website to get a sense of who might be in attendance and what the structure of the event is like.

Since you know what you're looking for and who you'd like to meet, you can quickly determine whether this event holds any potential. It does, so you put it in your calendar and schedule time a few days before to do further research and time within a day or two after to send your follow-up messages. The time set aside prior to the event allows you to research the organizers, presenters, awardees, and anyone else you think might be attending.

Armed with this information, you are getting quite excited about the event and go to sleep thinking about all the possibilities. Before leaving for the event, you review your Gmail canned responses to see if any of your follow-up email templates need to be updated and to remind yourself of the various projects you might bring up depending on who you end up meeting. You also double-check whether you have business cards with you and if they will be within easy reach.

You arrive at the conference just as it is getting started, which gives you a few minutes with the organizers before the crowd shows up. They ask how you heard about the event and you mention your colleague and one of your priority goals for attending. A thought sparks in the organizer, who says they will make an introduction for you when so-and-so arrives.

Feeling more confident you go to the breakfast buffet and have light conversation with a few people while waiting in line for coffee. One of those conversations leads to being invited to meet other people in the room. You are aware of your body language and make an effort to have an open stance so others can join your small circle of three. As others join your circle, you acknowledge them silently, and when there is a pause in the conversation, you briefly fill them in about what you had been discussing. Appreciative that you did this, the circle newcomers are interested in chatting with you further and ask what drew you to this event.

At one point, you find yourself in a conversation with only one other person, and you are momentarily nervous about how to wrap the conversation up gracefully. Then you remember you can ask for introductions. "I don't know many people here. Is there anyone you think I should meet?"

Using this method, you leapfrog through the crowd getting into better and better conversations because you are more confident and are being connected with the kind of people you really want to meet. Before each conversation comes to an end, you try to think of something to offer based on what had been discussed.

Then, if the conversation is going very well, you ask, "I'm trying to get more familiar with this industry. What other events would you suggest I attend?" Both this question and the one I mentioned a moment ago to wrap up gracefully gives the other person an opportunity to be a connector and share knowledge. This is a great way to make them feel good about themselves, and it also helps you either navigate the room or create a list of other possible events to attend.

As you collect business cards, you jot notes on them so you remember what you spoke about or what you offered to follow up about. You turn the corner down on the cards for your priority contacts you plan to reach out to when you get home. Since you drafted several email templates for follow-up messages, set aside time for follow up after the event, and had a system to track which business cards were a priority, you easily send all of your follow-up messages within an hour.

You make a note in your calendar to send a quick note to these contacts again next week with an article you think they'd like or another resource related to what you discussed. If it's someone you think has the potential to be a client, you add them to Contactually so you are sure not to lose touch between events.

You look up the dates of the events that were suggested to you and again set aside time before and after the event for research and follow up. When the next event comes up, you reach out to the people you met who you think might be attending, and you tell them you hope to cross paths again.

When you do cross paths, you are on your way to building a relationship which goes beyond simple transactions. Repeat this process, and you'll see results. You'll have stopped wasting time networking and now focus on building great relationships. Now you have a new definition of networking, one that is strategic, effective, and inclusive.

RESOURCES

Formatting Business Cards

What goes into the design and formatting of a business card is a personal choice, but there are some elements that should be considered.

Decide ahead of time what information to include on your business card to make it easier for new contacts to learn about you and your work. Job-hunting? Include your LinkedIn link. Are you a photographer? Include a link to your portfolio. Don't like to receive random calls on your cell phone? You have a few options. You can set up a Google Voice number, only list a landline, or leave a phone number off entirely so all inquiries have to go through your email.

Whatever links you include should be as professional looking as possible. Request a personalized LinkedIn URL (e.g., www.linkedin.com/in/robbiesamuels). The same is true for your email address. Do not use Hotmail, Yahoo, or dare I say an AOL account from twenty years ago. Ideally, you'll set up an email tied to your website. If you do not have a website, you can purchase a domain and have it point to your LinkedIn profile. If you're not ready to take this step, set up a Gmail account with your full name. Ideally, the name on your email would match the name on your LinkedIn personalized URL. Doing this will make the card look much more professional.

If this is a business card for a web-based business, individual consultant, or someone looking for work, then do not include a physical address. If you travel a lot or attend conferences several times a year, you may wish to put your city and state on the card.

I do not recommend using a non-standard size for your business card, as those are more difficult for the recipient to file and, in my experience, are more easily lost in the shuffle.

Please also avoid black backgrounds on both sides. This makes it difficult for the recipient to jot down a note as they receive your card—or you from jotting a note as you hand the card over. If you are featuring your photography or artwork on one side, then leave some white space on the other side. Early readers said they were curious what my business card looked like. Here it is: www.robbiesamuels.com/bizcard.

Bottom line, business cards are important. They also are not the point of networking. Consider them a means to an end. The goal is building a supportive network based on strong relationships.

HOW TO DRAFT FOLLOW-UP EMAIL BEFORE ATTENDING EVENT

To be prepared, write your follow-up email before going to the event. This will help you become more aware of who you want to meet and what your purpose is at the event. Having this pre-written increases the likelihood you will send a follow-up message—which is a critical part of networking.

Here are the specific steps to drafting this message:

Think about the people you'd like to meet at this event. This could be based on job titles, where they work, or any other demographics. If you are thinking about a specific person, then write this email draft with them in mind.

Imagine you met them and had a brief conversation at the event. You spent most of the conversation learning about them, by asking thoughtful questions. You had the opportunity to share a little bit about the work you do, and they seemed genuinely interested.

Now write the follow-up message you would send in this scenario. Include what you usually say about your work and then add a few more details you think they would find particularly interesting. Include links to your website or LinkedIn profile.

As I mentioned earlier, keep this message relatively brief, three short paragraphs or less. Sending longer messages often results in the recipient skimming, deciding this is an item they need to add to their to-do list, and then putting off responding. Be clear at the outset what you're asking for if you have a request.

Save this draft text so it's ready to be personalized after the event based on who you actually meet. If you are using Gmail, I highly recommend using Canned Responses to manage all of your draft follow-up messages so they are readily available when you're writing these emails. Not familiar with Canned Responses? I covered this Gmail Lab feature in the "Be Effective" section. Look for the "Using Technology" sub-header.

Steps to Host a Private Dinner at a Conference

Your job at conferences is to find your people, the people you can relate to and who you will want to stay in touch with after the event. It's a big crowd, so this might seem daunting, but you now have many tips and tools to help you find great connections.

One of the ways you can deepen your connection with colleagues and leaders in your field is to host a dinner when attending a conference. This is a great tip for anyone who has been attending the event for a few years and understands the value of being a host and convener.

Hosting a private dinner party during a conference doesn't need to be extravagant or expensive. It does require forethought and planning so the logistics are taken care of and the event runs smoothly. Beyond logistics, paying close attention to the experience your guests are having and how welcomed they feel is key.

If you've attended this conference in prior years, then you probably went home with a stack of business cards. Whether you followed up with people right after the event or not, review this stack and identify people you'd like to see again. Even if you find just three people you'd want to invite—you have the start to a dinner party.

If you are nervous about lining up seven to nine guests to join you for dinner, identify a co-host. This co-host can be a close colleague or someone you've met a few times and enjoyed their company. Each of you invites half the guests for a dinner party of eight to ten people. Counting the two of you, this means each of you invites three or four guests.

Logistics:

1. Decide a few weeks prior to the conference you want to host a dinner.

2. Identify and confirm a co-host (optional).

3. Review the conference schedule to find a time for dinner that isn't competing with major programming (ideally toward the end of the conference).

4. Select a nearby restaurant which:

    a. can host a group of eight to ten people (keep it to at most ten people including yourself)

    b. is relatively quiet

    c. doesn't have TVs on in every direction

d. has menu options for a wide range of dietary restrictions/preferences

e. will split the check so each person receives their own (ideal)

5. Identify at least three people to invite before the conference, likely people you've met in previous years. Reach out to them, remind them you met last year, and let them know you're putting together a small dinner party during the conference.

6. Keep the invite short and simple. Confirm two or three guests prior the conference. This will give you more confidence when inviting others you connect with at the event.

7. Invite additional guests throughout the event until you have a max of 10 people, including you and your co-host.

8. Ask for everyone's cell number as you confirm their attendance, so if plans change you can easily send reminders and updates. Be sure everyone has your cell number as well.

9. Once everyone has arrived and ordered, give each guest a few minutes to introduce themselves. Include a question related to the event,

such as, "What inspiration are you looking for this year?" or "What was one of your take-aways thus far?"

Lightly facilitate to encourage interesting conversation and connections among your guests. When guests find an uncommon commonality you will be appreciated as the host who brought them together.

EMAIL INTRO ETIQUETTE

Networking isn't about collecting business cards; it's about building relationships. One way to do this is to make introductions between two people who may benefit from knowing each other. Sometimes you come up with the idea to introduce two people. Sometimes you are asked to make an introduction on someone's behalf.

Before making an email introduction stop to consider whether the connection will be beneficial for both parties. If not, then it's probably best not to make the introduction because your aim should be that both parties are happy you introduced them. If you are unsure whether the more senior person would be open to the introduction, it is best to email them privately to ask. Give them a gracious way to decline and don't be surprised if they say no or don't respond.

**Busy people stay productive
because they know how to say no.**

Asking To Be Introduced?
If you are the one asking to be introduced, save the connector a lot of time and send them a thoughtfully written, and brief, bio and a description of what you'd like them to share in an introduction. This will make it a lot easier for the connector to act on your request and

prevent it from becoming a "to-do" item on their already too long to-do list. If you put the onus on the connector, the chances of the email being sent is greatly reduced.

If this connection would be beneficial to both parties, take the time to write a thoughtful introduction email.

In the subject line: *E-intro Bob Jones and Marie Vantos.* Include both names in the subject line to increase the chances of the email being opened.

In the first paragraph: *Bob, I want to introduce you to Marie Vantos.* Follow this with a sentence about who Marie is, how you met, and/or how well you know each other. *Marie, meet Bob Jones.* Follow this with a sentence about who Bob is, how you met, and/or how well you know each other.

In the second paragraph: In one or two sentences share how the introduction occurred to you. This is a nice touch, as it gives both parties context right away about why you thought they should meet.

Have they already met? Mention this so both parties are reminded and no one is embarrassed for forgetting a brief prior introduction.

In the third paragraph: Write a complimentary (but not inaccurate) sentence about each party. Share their strengths and accomplishments. Include a link to each person's website, blog, or LinkedIn profile. When done well this section makes it clear why they should connect and makes the idea enticing. End this paragraph with an explicit statement: *This is why I think the two of you should meet...*

In the fourth brief paragraph: Make a specific recommendation about how they should connect. Should they meet over coffee? Schedule lunch? Connect over the phone or Skype?

Being specific will help them move to the next step. It also suggests how much effort you're encouraging them to make for their first meeting. Scheduling lunch would be more involved than a phone call, so you'd hesitate to suggest this unless you believe it is in both of their best interests.

If their time zones are different, be sure to mention where each party lives so that is factored in when scheduling.

In the final paragraph: *Let me know when you two connect.*

Before you hit send: Be sure you're not accidentally forwarding an email chain which will be embarrassing to either party. Either delete the prior thread or edit it.

If either party has an assistant who handles scheduling meetings, you may want to include them on this email.

What Happens Next?

Okay, so now that the intro email has been sent. What happens next?

Generally, the first person to respond to an email introduction is the less senior person. This isn't always the case, as someone with more experience might respond quickly because of their relationship with the person making the connection. Either way, move the connector's email to BCC. Then in the first line thank the connector for making the introduction and mention you put them in the BCC to save their inbox. This means the connector will get an email letting them know there was an initial response, but not be cc'd on all subsequent emails to coordinate a time to meet.

This initial BCC email is not the same thing as closing the loop about what happened. This email should be sent after you meet. Another update should be sent if you two do some business together later on.

If this becomes a valuable contact, such as a big client of yours, send a thank you gift to the connector (a gift basket, bottle of wine, tickets to a game or the theatre). Going the extra mile to thank them will make you memorable, and they will be on the lookout for other quality introductions among their network.

CONTACTUALLY

To help me manage my most meaningful relationships and the ones I hope will become significant I use Contactually, a robust CRM perfect for managing my professional network.

I put each contact into a "bucket" which correlates to how frequently I want to be in touch. When this amount of time has passed, if I have not reconnected, the contact's name appears on my dashboard.

What I appreciate most about Contactually is it helps me stay in touch with my weakest links: the contacts where I don't have a specific project to work together on, but I value what they do and don't want them to slip away.

Sign up for a free trial by using my affiliate link: www.robbiesamuels.com/contactually. Let me know if you do, and I'll help you get set up for success.

Dux-Soup

The Chrome plug-in Dux-Soup integrates with LinkedIn and enables you to tag profiles and write private notes. With this plug-in, LinkedIn once again becomes a simple contact relationship management (CRM) tool. There is a free option that lets you write notes for every profile you visit.

In addition, the paid version allows you to download a spreadsheet that includes the tags and notes for your priority contacts. For instance, if you were creating a shortlist of people you hope to stay in touch with after a conference. You could tag those profiles, write a brief note, and then view them periodically. This keeps those contacts from getting lost among the rest of your connections.

If you have a free LinkedIn account and have found it difficult to track your top contacts, you should consider the professional Dux-Soup package.

As an affiliate, I'm able to share a special offer – 6-month package includes one month free or 12-month package includes three months free. Learn more at www.robbiesamuels.com/dux-soup.

Notes

1. Tiziana Casciaro , Francesca Gino, and Maryam Kouchaki, "The Contaminating Effects of Building Instrumental Ties: How Networking Can Make Us Feel Dirty," <u>Harvard Business School</u>, April 24, 2014, accessed May 29, 2017.

2. <u>On the Schmooze</u>, "Conditions of Satisfaction," interview, March 27, 2017: www.robbiesamuels.com/2017/03/ots-037-conditions-of-satisfaction-jeffrey-hayzlett, accessed May 29, 2017.

3. <u>On the Schmooze</u>, "Act with Integrity," interview, November 22, 2016: www.robbiesamuels.com/2016/11/ots-021-act-with-integrity-dr-josh-packard, accessed May 29, 2017

4. <u>On the Schmooze</u>, "Believe in the Power of Your Network," interview, February 28, 2017: www.robbiesamuels.com/2017/02/ots-033-believe-in-the-power-of-your-network-john-corcoran, accessed May 29, 2017.

5. <u>On the Schmooze</u>, "Propel Your Career," interview, January, 31, 2017: www.robbiesamuels.com/2017/01/ots-029-propel-your-career-howard-putnam-csp, accessed May 29, 2017

6. "Propel Your Career."

7. Dale Carnegie, *How to Win Friends and Influence People*, Revised Edition (New York: Simon and Schuster, 1981).

8. <u>On the Schmooze</u>, "Change Master," interview, April 11, 2017: www.robbiesamuels.com/2017/04/ots-039-change-master-stephanie-chung, accessed May 29, 2017.

9. "Change Master."

10. "Change Master."

11. Michael Ansaldo, "5 cool ways to use business cards in Evernote," PC World, May 14, 2014, accessed May 29, 2017.

12. On the Schmooze, "Thought(ful) Leaders," interview, March 14, 2017: www.robbiesamuels.com/2017/03/ots-035-thoughtful-leaders-susan-roane, accessed May 29, 2017.

13. "Thought(ful) Leaders."

14. Interview [unpublished], Robbie Samuels, recorded March 28, 2017.

15. Interview [unpublished], Robbie Samuels, recorded March 28, 2017.

16. On the Schmooze, "Moral Authority," interview, February 14, 2017: www.robbiesamuels.com/2017/02/ots-031-moral-authority-dorie-clark, accessed May 29, 2017.

17. "Moral Authority."

18. "Moral Authority."

19. On the Schmooze, "Change that sticks," interview, December 6, 2016: www.robbiesamuels.com/2016/12/ots-023-change-that-sticks-chris-clarke-epstein, accessed May 29, 2017.

20. On the Schmooze, "Speak with Conviction," interview, May 23, 2017: www.robbiesamuels.com/2017/05/ots-045-speak-with-conviction-scott-stratten, accessed May 29, 2017.

21. "Speak with Conviction."

22. Interview [unpublished], Robbie Samuels, recorded June 9, 2017.

23. Interview [unpublished], Robbie Samuels, recorded June 9, 2017.

24. Ramit Sethi, "The Productivity System I Built to Stay in Touch with People," I Will Teach You to Be Rich, accessed May 29, 2017.

25. Nicubunu. Woman Silhouette 02. 2015. Clipart. OpenClipArt, www.openclipart.org/detail/14065/woman-silhouette-02.

26. Wood, Margana. Business Man Standing Silhouette in Black and White Image. 2011. Clipart. Clker, www.clker.com/clipart-140575.html.

27. Red X. Clipart. Dr. Odd, www.drodd.com/html7/red-x.html.

28. Fed. Young Man Silhouette Graphics. Clipart. Silhouette Graphics, www.silhouettegraphics.net/young-man-silhouette-graphics.

29. Chisty, Zeshan. Dark Green Check Mark. 2013. Clipart. Clker, www.clker.com/clipart-dark-green-check-mark-3.html.

30. Beryl. 2 o'clock. 2013. Clipart. Cliker, http://www.clker.com/clipart-2-o-clock-.html.

31. Hate Clipart No Red Circle. Clipart. Clipart All, www.clipartall.com/image.php?id=192135.

32. [Silhouette Footprints]. Clipart. Pixel Bay, www.pixabay.com/en/toes-foot-feet-silhouette-150216.

33. Lauren Easton, "Making a case for singular 'they,'" AP Blog, March 24, 2017, accessed May 29, 2017

34. Nate Riggs, "An Interesting Twist on Being a Conference 'VIP,'" LinkedIn Pulse, March 22, 2016, accessed May 29, 2017.

35. Interview [unpublished], Robbie Samuels, recorded April 28, 2017.

36. Interview [unpublished], Robbie Samuels, recorded May 4, 2017.

37. Interview [unpublished], Robbie Samuels, recorded May 4, 2017.

38. Interview [unpublished], Robbie Samuels, recorded April 28, 2017

39. Interview [unpublished], Robbie Samuels, recorded May 4, 2017.

Acknowledgments

My experience organizing Socializing for Justice inspired this book. SoJust is a grassroots, cross-cultural, cross-issue, progressive community and network in Boston that I founded in 2006. About a year after forming this Meetup group, we gathered our regular attendees together to discuss how to make sure we continued to be a welcoming and inclusive organization. I knew over time groups become very cliquey and it is particularly difficult for newcomers to feel welcomed if long-time attendees are always huddled together ignoring them.

So I asked this group of about 20 regular attendees if they would be willing to arrive 15 minutes early to greet newcomers who show up early and stand around awkwardly while I'm putting the finishing touches on the event. No problem said these regulars. I asked them to help out at the front door—signing people in and generally greeting them. Again, they said no problem. Then I asked if they would also mingle and work the room. And that's when I got a lot of deer in headlights looks instead of agreement.

Because Socializing for Justice had been so welcoming, we had attracted quite a few shy and/or introverted people as regulars. While they appreciated the welcoming spirit of our group and wanted to pay it forward, they did not feel comfortable with the idea of mingling. It was way out of their comfort zone.

Soon after this discussion I started to offer a session called Art of the Schmooze. By 2009, this became my signature session and I began to be paid to speak. Thus began my side hustle as a speaker—and my topics grew to include Fundraising: Getting Past the Fear of Asking, Intercultural Communication, and Mentors Make a Difference: Build Your Personal Board of Directors, to name a few.

In 2014, I left my career organizing fundraising events and working with major donors to pursue being a professional speaker full-time. I had no idea how much my life would change because of founding Socializing for Justice and that conversation with our regulars.

The launch of this book coincides with the close of Socializing for Justice after 11 years, 3100+ members, 230+ events, and countless connections. I am indebted to all of the SoJust STARZ (aka regulars) and in particular wish to acknowledge my co-founder Hilary Allen, co-organizers Alison Brill and Jessica "JC" Critcher, and ProfDev Coordinator Mark Williams. They each stepped up into a volunteer leadership role to keep the group going and growing. It is through this group that I learned so much about radical inclusion, creating a welcoming community, and strategies for turning first-timers into long-time attendees.

Soon after leaving my career to become a solopreneur, I joined the National Speakers Association and attended my first Influence conference. That first year I set a goal to return a year later having launched a podcast and qualify as a professional member—and that is exactly what I did. At my second conference I set a goal to return having written a book—and you are reading proof I met that goal too. The expertise and encouragement I've received from this stellar group of fellow speakers has kept me motivated as I learned what it means to run my own business.

Through the National Speakers Association I met Jeffrey Hayzlett, whom I later interviewed and included in this book. Since he invited me to join C-Suite Radio I've had access to a much wider array of authors and experts to interview on my podcast. Many of whom are mentioned in this book.

The idea to host a podcast at all was inspired by Pat Flynn, host of Smart Passive Income podcast. I listened to most of his archived episodes during the first six months of being a solopreneur and learned so much—

including that I needed to stop consuming and start producing my own content.

Finding time to launch a podcast when I was expecting my first son was not easy. So I made launching a podcast my leadership commitment when I was graduating from LeadBoston, a senior executive leadership program organized by YW Boston. Many of my early guests were fellow alums of this 25+ year organization and JoAnn Cox '15 was one of my early readers for this book. To make my podcast a reality, I signed up for the Show-Runner podcast course and received guidance from experienced podcast hosts.

I'm acknowledging all of the people who helped me launch my podcast because this is how I met many of the people who shared their insights in this book. Hosting a podcast, and interviewing guests, has helped me broaden and deepen my professional network. It has been a source of professional development as well, with all of the great takeaways I've learned and shared with my listeners. This book would not have as many illustrative stories and quotes if I had not hosted On the Schmooze.

I also must thank Dorie Clark for being my good friend and mentor for many years. If it were up to her I would have progressed much faster along my path to author, professional speaker, and business owner. Watching her excel in her career has been an inspiration. I'm so pleased I joined her Recognized Expert course, where I met several fantastic members who have been a huge part of my book writing and launching process. Shout out in particular to Marlena Corcoran, Liz Kauffmann, and Aleksandr Zhuk for their writing feedback.

Dorie's course is also where I met Melissa Smith, who has been my SPS accountability partner and helped me find Teri Pastorino, my amazing virtual assistant. SPS community as a whole has been a wonderful resource as a first-time author. It turns out writing the book is really only the first step. Thankfully Melissa and the SPS community guided me along the rest of the way to launch day.

Speaking of accountability partners, I've surrounded myself with smart people who have pushed me to be my best self. Regular check-ins with my accountability partners has kept me on track despite being a work-at-home dad with a toddler. Thank you to Chris West, Darnell Moses, and Steven Dry. I've also received a lot of encouragement and wise advice from a monthly networking/mastermind/accountability dinner that I host. This began as a gathering of Ramit's Brain Trust members in the Boston area and when RBT closed membership was expanded to include Boston area members of Recognized Expert and SPS. I love being around people who invest in their professional and personal development.

It seriously takes a village to balance being a successful business owner and engaged at-home parent. Part of our village has been a slew of Simmons College students who have taken my son out for fun adventures—giving me time to work on my business. Thank you in particular to Amanda Farrington for stepping up this summer. Our babysitters will become even more essential after my second son is born in December 2017.

Other members of my village include: Iris Polit Di Paola, whom I've known since high school, has been pushing me to write a book for over a decade. If it were up to her it would be a memoir titled "Self Made Man." Since 2000, Robbii Wessen has been sharing his graphic design skill and making me look good.

My entrepreneurial spirit was evident even when I was a little tyke and I am deeply grateful my mom and dad encouraged me to live my full potential.

My wife, Jess Samuels, also saw this potential and is the real reason I've been able to leave the daily grind and pursue my dream as a solopreneur professional speaker, podcast host, coach, and now author. She shared her graphic design skills, editing feedback, and always shifting co-parenting duty as tangible evidence of her support. She also paid our bills while I slowly and thoughtfully got clarity around the business I wanted to build and whom I wanted to serve. Without her deep and unwavering support I would not be able to change the lives of so many clients and readers.

And last, but definitely not least, thank you as a whole to my Launch Team members—over 300 people signed up to help make this book a huge success.

About the Author

ROBBIE SAMUELS has been recognized as a networking expert by *Inc.* and *Lifehacker*, and profiled in *Stand Out: How to Find Your Breakthrough Idea and Build a Following Around It* by Dorie Clark.

A professional member of the National Speakers Association, the common thread through all of his talks is relationship building—whether through networking, fundraising, sales, or diversity & inclusion. He has presented to audiences in many different fields, including Marriott International, PA Consulting, AmeriCorps VISTA, and the Gay & Lesbian Medical Association.

While practical and filled with easy to implement action steps, his talks are most often described as "dynamic, engaging, and funny." He shares "small, big ideas," everyday ideas, which are accessible and immediately actionable, and have the power to inspire significant change.

Samuels taught at Lesley College, and guest lectured at Babson College, Boston Architectural College, Brandeis University, Cornell University, Curry College, Lasell College, Roger Williams University, and Tufts University.

In addition to speaking, he shares his personal brand of inclusive networking strategies as a coach. His one-on-one coaching clients and virtual group coaching program members move from feeling anxious and/or disillusioned by networking to feeling strategic, effective, and empowered.

Samuels is the host of On the Schmooze, a weekly podcast which features interviews with talented people from different fields who share untold stories of leadership and networking. Put his takeaways at the end of each interview into practice this week and benefit from them for years to come.

Listen to his podcast at www.OntheSchmooze.com, iTunes, and Stitcher.

Visit www.RobbieSamuels.com to book Robbie Samuels for your next event or to request an interview.

Follow him on www.twitter.com/robbiesamuels for more networking tips and resources to help you succeed.

Author photo by: Maureen Cotton Photography

Thumbs Up or Thumbs Down?

THANK YOU for reading this book! I would love to hear from you. Writing an Amazon review is as easy as answering any of these questions:

- What did you enjoy about the book?
- What is your most valuable takeaway or insight?
- What have you done differently—or what will you do differently—because of what you read?
- To whom would you recommend this book?

Seriously, just two or three sentences would be amazing. Your feedback helps to get this book into the hands of those who need it most.

I look forward to hearing what resonated with you.

Thank you in advance,
Robbie

Thank you for purchasing the
print version of this book,
I'm bundling it with the audio
book at no extra charge.

Download at www.RobbieSamuels.com/audiobook

43976865R00110

Made in the USA
Middletown, DE
04 May 2019